GRIT AND
AND

Grace

GRIT AND GRACE

GRIT AND GRACE

GRIT AND GRACE

DEDICATION

This book is dedicated to every inspiring woman—past, present, and future—who has dared to dream, to rise, and to make a difference. To the trailblazers who have shattered ceilings, the quiet warriors who have fought battles unseen, and the everyday heroes who lift others as they climb—this is for you.

To the mothers, daughters, sisters, and friends who remind us of our strength, to the mentors who believe in us before we believe in ourselves, and to the fearless women who lead with heart and courage—your impact is immeasurable, and your legacy will live on.

And to the families of the incredible authors in this book— thank you for your unwavering support, your encouragement, and your love. Behind every powerful woman is a network of people who cheer her on, pick her up, and remind her she is capable of anything.

This book is not just a collection of stories—it is a celebration of resilience, passion, and the unstoppable force of women standing together.

CONTENTS

FOREWORD

BY TRACEY MUNRO

Welcome to this incredible celebration of women, a collection that sparkles with stories, wisdom, and inspiration from remarkable women around the globe.

International Women's Day isn't just a date in the calendar; it's a movement, a reminder, and, frankly, a call to action. It's a day where we pause—not to rest—but to raise our voices, clap for each other, and dream a little louder. It's about honouring the progress we've made, acknowledging the battles still to be fought, and standing together with unshakable determination.

This book is a testament to the strength, courage, and

resilience of women everywhere. Within these pages, you'll meet trailblazers who have turned challenges into stepping stones, fears into fire, and ideas into impact. These women have navigated paths that weren't always paved, carving out their own space in industries, communities, and causes that matter. They have faced adversity with unwavering resolve, proving that true power lies not in the absence of struggle but in the refusal to be defeated by it. But let's be clear—this isn't about perfection; it's about perseverance. It's about showing up, even when the odds look less than friendly. It's about daring to be seen and heard in a world that's still catching up to the brilliance of what women can do. It's about lifting each other up, amplifying each other's voices, and rewriting the narrative for future generations.

So, as you turn these pages, let their stories spark something in you—a smile, a moment of reflection, or even the nudge you need to take that leap you've been hesitating over. Let their words remind you that you are capable, worthy, and powerful beyond measure.

To every woman reading this: your story matters, your voice counts, and your dreams are valid. Stand tall, shine bright, and never dim your light for anyone. The world needs your brilliance, your passion, and your courage.

You are not alone on this journey. You are part of a sisterhood—one that thrives on lifting each other up, celebrating each other's victories, and holding space for one another in moments of doubt. When one of us rises, we all rise. So, dare to dream boldly, speak fearlessly, and embrace every part of who you are.

GRIT AND GRACE

Here's to us—women supporting women, breaking barriers, and redefining what's possible. Together, we are a force of nature, unstoppable in our pursuit of greatness. Let's inspire, empower, and create a future where every woman knows her worth and wields her power unapologetically.

The world is waiting for your magic. Let's go make it happen.

Happy reading and Happy International Women's Day!

With love, success, and unbreakable sisterhood,

Tracey x

Connect with me:

Facebook: www.facebook.com/traceymunro12/

Website: www.propublishinghouse.com

GRIT AND GRACE

"SHE IS UNSTOPPABLE—NOT BECAUSE SHE NEVER STUMBLES, BUT BECAUSE SHE RISES EVERY TIME WITH MORE STRENGTH, MORE WISDOM, AND MORE GRACE."

Tracey Munro

GRIT AND GRACE

CHAPTER 1

My Voice: A Journey to Empowerment

BY AMY MOSTERT

"What if you never show up for your own life?"

The first time I heard this, it hit me like a tonne of bricks. I couldn't shake it. What if I wasn't showing up for my life? What if I was only showing up for the things I thought I *had* to do, instead of the ones that made me feel alive? What if I was showing up for everyone else but barely showing up for *me*?

That question planted itself in my mind and didn't leave. It shook me, but in the best way. It was the moment something inside me clicked. I started to see things differently and started to see *myself* differently. And it felt like I'd been waiting for that moment my whole life.

For so long, I felt out of place, like I was stuck on the outside looking in. I tried to fit into spaces that never felt quite right, wearing masks to blend in and pretending I wasn't struggling. Deep down though, I always knew I was 'different'. I just didn't know why. It wasn't until much later that I realised those feelings weren't a weakness, they were part of what made me *me*.

Now, I carry a mantra with me: *Veni, Vidi, Vici.* I came, I saw, I conquered. It's a reminder that no matter how hard life gets, no matter how heavy the weight feels, I can keep moving forward. Sometimes that forward motion is messy and slow. Sometimes it's more like crawling than conquering. But the point is, I keep going.

And that's what I want for you too. Life throws us all challenges, and it's easy to feel like those struggles define us. But they don't. They're just chapters in the story, and *you* get to decide how the story goes.

So let me ask you: What lessons have your struggles taught you about your own strength? How can you embrace *your* story and start showing up for *your* life?

I've learned that those moments of isolation and doubt weren't the end, they were the beginning. They taught me to see the light within myself. To embrace it. And most importantly, to keep showing up.

I am me.

I am enough.

I am worthy.

I deserve it all.

And I can have it.

The Foundation of Me

"Our childhood writes the opening chapters of our story, but it is our choices and dreams that shape the ending."

Childhood is often painted as a time of simplicity and joy, but for me, it felt more like walking a tightrope between belonging and isolation. I had friends, and there were moments of laughter and fun, but these were often overshadowed by a lingering sense of being on the outside. I always felt different, like I wasn't enough or like I didn't quite measure up to the other friends in the group.

I became an expert at adapting myself to fit in, mimicking their behaviours, adopting their likes, and even downplaying my achievements to avoid outshining them. It was exhausting, and while I wanted to belong, I often found myself wondering why it never felt quite right. Even in those moments when I was part of a group, there was a sadness, a sense of being left out, of not fully fitting in, as if I was living on the edges of their friendships rather than at the heart of them.

Yet amidst the challenges, there was one constant that brought me joy: learning. Even back then, I loved discovering new information; it felt like I was gaining knowledge and, with it, a sense of power and purpose. I was drawn to helping people, whether it was solving their problems or making them feel better with the insights I'd gained. It gave me a sense of connection and fulfilment that friendships alone couldn't always provide. It was my way of contributing, even when I felt on the outside.

When I was diagnosed with a chronic illness at 15, it only added to the complexities. Suddenly, the energy it took to maintain these friendships, already a challenge, became overwhelming. Cancelling plans, missing out, and struggling to keep up left me feeling guilt-ridden, as though I was failing as a friend. It was yet another way I felt set apart from my peers.

Looking back now, through the lens of neurodivergence, so much of my childhood and teen years makes sense. The struggles with fitting in, the emotional exhaustion of masking my true self, and the sense of being different weren't signs of failure, they were parts of who I am. My love of learning and helping others, which started so early in life, became key elements of my identity and a source of strength. I can now see that those experiences, while painful, shaped me into the resilient and self-aware person I am today.

Childhood and friendships are complex, often filled with moments of growth, pain, and joy intertwined. While it's unfortunate that these challenges were a part of my journey, they've helped me see the importance of embracing who I truly am.

Empowerment Tip

Reflect on your own friendships and childhood experiences.

What did they teach you about yourself? How can you show compassion for the person you were then, navigating a world that often felt confusing or isolating? And now, how can you use those lessons to embrace the unique and powerful person you've become?

Finding Strength Through Struggles

"Sometimes the bravest thing you can do is simply show up for yourself, even when the world feels too heavy."

My school and college years were a confusing blend of highs and lows, moments of trying to fit in and times when I felt deeply out of place. I wanted to belong, to find my place among my peers, but I was also grappling with struggles that I couldn't yet name. Unbeknownst to me, these experiences weren't just shaping my identity, they were profoundly impacting my nervous system and laying the groundwork for the chronic illness I would later come to understand.

Every day, I navigated the social pressures of school, trying to conform to the expectations of those around me. I desperately wanted to fit in, but it often felt like I was running a race I wasn't equipped to compete in. Behind the scenes, I was unknowingly masking my neurodivergence and chronic illness symptoms, constantly ignoring the signals my body and mind were sending me.

This relentless push to meet external expectations was deeply dysregulating to my nervous system. At the time, I didn't realise the toll this was taking on my body. The stress of trying to keep up, the anxiety of feeling misunderstood, and the fear of rejection created a cycle of physical and emotional exhaustion. My body was in a state of fight-or-flight far too often, though I wouldn't come to understand this dynamic for many years.

I vividly recall a time when I stood up for myself in my later years in education, confronting a group of friends who had dismissed me and my feelings. Though it felt empowering to finally speak my truth, their response left me more isolated than ever. The rejection that followed was devastating, and the stress of losing friendships only added to the strain on my nervous system.

At the time, I blamed myself for the fallout, unable to see that I was advocating for my own worth. Now, I recognise that those relationships weren't healthy. But back then, the emotional weight of these experiences piled on top of the physical toll of chronic illness, leaving me depleted in ways I couldn't yet articulate.

The nervous system dysregulation I experienced wasn't just a fleeting response to difficult situations, it became a chronic state. The constant effort to mask my struggles, keep up with peers, and endure unkind treatment from others left me in a state of perpetual stress. This dysregulation fed into the symptoms of my chronic illness, making it harder to recover from even small setbacks and leaving me in a cycle of physical and emotional imbalance.

The impact on my mental health was equally profound. I wasn't just tired; I was burnt out. The untreated mental health challenges I faced only deepened my sense of isolation, and instead of seeking help, I turned to coping mechanisms that numbed the pain but did nothing to address the root cause.

Despite these challenges, some moments reminded me I was capable of more than just surviving. Becoming a published poet was one of those moments, a validation that my voice and creativity mattered.

My academic accomplishments and achievements, and the praise received from my teachers and tutors, inspired me and motivated me to keep going and to keep striving for excellence in my future.

Another unexpected event came during a holiday when I was selected as a finalist in a modelling competition. It was entirely out of my comfort zone, but for a brief moment, it allowed me to step into a version of myself that felt bold and seen. These experiences, though fleeting, were anchors that kept me moving forward.

It would take years for me to fully understand how much my nervous system had been affected during these formative years. I now see how the constant stress, masking, and internalised feelings of inadequacy fed into my chronic illness and kept me from being in optimal physical and mental health. What I once saw as personal failures were, in fact, the natural responses of a body and mind under constant strain.

Through education, introspection, and self-compassion, I've learned to reframe these experiences. I understand now that my body was trying to communicate with me all along, asking for rest, care, and understanding.

These words—*I came, I saw, I conquered*—capture how I view those years now. I came through challenges I didn't yet have the tools to understand. I saw the lessons hidden in the struggles. And I conquered the belief that those years defined my worth.

Empowerment Tip

"Your body is your greatest ally. When you learn to listen to its whispers, you can heal what you once thought was unchangeable."

Take a moment to reflect on how your body and mind responded to past struggles. If you've ever felt stuck or drained, it wasn't weakness—it was your nervous system protecting you in the only way it knew how. With understanding and compassion, you can begin to unravel those patterns and find balance again.

Standing in My Power

"She remembered who she was, and the game changed."– Lalah Delia

There's a unique kind of freedom in finally seeing yourself for who you are and embracing every piece of it—the victories, the struggles, the quirks, and the lessons learned. For me, standing in my power today means celebrating my neurodiversity and chronic illness as essential, even beautiful, parts of my story. These aren't hurdles to overcome; they're strengths to harness, insights to offer, and perspectives that allow me to connect with others on a deeper level.

In both The Ops Ladies and Mum Wife Warrior, I've found ways to weave every part of myself into the businesses and communities I build. With The Ops Ladies, I embrace my strategic mind, my ability to see systems and solutions where others see chaos. This side of me thrives on structure, organisation, and the joy of seeing a client transform their business from overwhelming to thriving. But the Mum Wife Warrior in me brings something different: vulnerability, compassion, and the ability to meet people where they are. Together, these two sides aren't in conflict—they're a powerful combination that allows me to create spaces where others feel seen, understood, and empowered.

For years, I thought I needed to conform—to think like others, act like others, and fit into a mould that simply wasn't designed for me. But I've learned that my neurodivergence isn't a barrier; it's my secret weapon. It helps me see patterns others might miss, find creative solutions to complex problems, and approach challenges with a perspective that's entirely my own.

One recent moment stands out: A client came to me overwhelmed by their growing business. They felt stuck, lost in a sea of to-do lists and expectations. Drawing on my experiences—and the unique way my brain works—I mapped out a clear path forward. I used both the logical, systems-driven side of my mind and the compassionate understanding of someone who's been there. Together, we not only found solutions but also reignited their passion for what they do.

"I came, I saw, I conquered." As I said earlier in this chapter, this phrase has become a mantra for me, guiding the way I approach every challenge. Whether it's setting boundaries in my personal life, standing up for what I believe in, or

advocating for someone else who feels unseen, I lean into this mindset every day.

One of the most powerful ways I've embodied this spirit was advocating for a fellow business owner struggling with self-doubt. They reminded me so much of myself in earlier years—unsure if their voice was enough, unsure if they deserved to take up space. I shared my story, not as someone who's figured it all out, but as someone who's walked a similar path. By helping them see their worth, I also reaffirmed my own.

One of the greatest lessons I've learned is that I don't have to do it all alone. Communities like The Ops Ladies and Mum Wife Warrior have shown me the beauty of connection—of working alongside like-minded people who accept all of me, just as I accept all of them. Together, we create something far greater than any of us could alone.

When I work with others, I bring not just my skills but also my story. I bring the compassion and understanding I wish someone had shown me years ago. I bring the knowledge and lessons that only come from living through the hard stuff. This isn't about perfection; it's about showing up authentically and creating a safe space for others to do the same.

Standing in my power today means honouring my journey. It means using everything I've learned—the highs and the lows—to create businesses, communities, and a life that feels deeply aligned with who I am. It's about rejecting the pressure to conform and instead embracing authenticity as the ultimate success.

To anyone reading this, my advice is simple: Redefine what

success looks like for you. You don't need to fit in to belong. You don't need to have all the answers to take the next step. And you don't need to go it alone.

Empowerment Tip

Take a moment to reflect on your own journey. What parts of yourself have you been hiding, dismissing, or trying to change? Those might just be your greatest strengths. Embrace them and watch how the game changes.

You've got this.

The Ongoing Journey

Looking forward, I am filled with optimism, knowing that every step on my journey has brought me closer to a deeper understanding of myself. Embracing my neurodiversity and navigating my health challenges have empowered me not just to survive but to thrive. They've encouraged me to dream bigger and act with intention.

Veni, Vidi, Vici remains my guiding light. It reminds me that fears are meant to be faced, and meaningful goals are meant to be pursued, no matter how daunting they seem.

As I continue on this journey, I envision a life where I inspire others through everything I do. Whether it's sharing my story, supporting others as they navigate their challenges, or creating resources that empower them, I am committed to helping others see the beauty in their own unique paths.

Understanding myself more deeply has given me a resilience I never thought possible. Life's uncertainties no longer feel like threats but opportunities to adapt, grow, and thrive.

Most importantly, I've learned that life is an ongoing journey with no fixed destination. It's not about arriving at a place of perfection but about continually evolving, learning, and embracing every twist and turn with grace and courage.

When I look to the future, I see endless opportunities for growth, both personally and professionally. I am excited by the unknown because it holds the promise of discovery. Meeting new people, learning new lessons, and embracing new experiences will shape me into an even better version of myself.

I know I've come so far, but I also know there's so much further to go. And I welcome it. Every new chapter, every new challenge, and every new victory is an invitation to grow.

Empowerment Tip

Set bold goals, even if they feel out of reach. Understand that setbacks are not failures; they are stepping stones. Each one brings you closer to the person you are becoming. Empowerment is not a moment; it's a process, a journey you are constantly walking. Write down your goals or create a vision board to begin to manifest your future.

Your Turn to Shine

"What if you never show up for your own life?"

As I reach the end of this chapter, I find myself holding onto this question, not as a lingering doubt but as a reminder of the power of choosing myself every single day. It wasn't always this way. For years, I lived a version of my life muted by expectations, of others and myself. But understanding myself has allowed me to show up for myself in ways I never thought possible.

Empowerment isn't a straight line, and it's not a destination. It's a choice. A daily choice. Some days, it's easy, like taking a deep breath and stepping into alignment with my purpose. On other days, it's the quiet defiance of honouring my boundaries, even when it feels uncomfortable. But every single day, it's about owning my story and living life on my terms.

Not long ago, I experienced one of those moments where everything clicked—a feeling of being truly aligned with my purpose. It wasn't a grand achievement or a public milestone; it was a quiet morning with a cup of coffee in hand, reflecting on how far I'd come. It was in that stillness that I realised the power of showing up for myself, of not apologising for who I am, but celebrating it. Moments like these are the culmination of years of learning and unlearning. They're the result of advice like the "let them theory" letting people be who they are and focusing on who I want to be. It's the wisdom of recognising my inner badass, the voice that says, "*I am capable. I am worthy. I am enough.*"

You might be reading this, wondering where to begin. My journey wasn't perfect, and yours won't be either. But that's the beauty of it. Empowerment isn't about perfection; it's about progress. It's about embracing your struggles, your differences, and the pieces of yourself you've been hiding. Those parts of you are not weaknesses, they're your superpowers.

Ask yourself this: Where are you holding back in your life? Where are you not showing up for yourself? Maybe it's in a relationship, a career choice, or the way you speak to yourself. Start small. Write your thoughts in a journal. Set one boundary. Celebrate one part of yourself you've kept hidden.

Here's my mantra, and maybe it can become yours too: *I am not my fears; I am my dreams.*

A Final Thought

Your voice matters. Your story is valuable. You are more resilient than you know, and the challenges you face are simply stepping stones to your greatness.

So, take that first step. Show up for yourself. Shine. Because this is your life, and it's your turn to live it fully.

What if you never show up for your own life?

Don't let that be your story. Instead, let today be the moment you choose to embrace it all and write a new one.

Connect with me

Linktree: https://linktr.ee/amymostert

"OUR CHILDHOOD WRITES THE
OPENING CHAPTERS OF OUR STORY,
BUT IT IS OUR CHOICES AND DREAMS
THAT SHAPE THE ENDING."

Amy Mostert

CHAPTER 2

The power of showing up!

BY CAROLINE MARTIN

Back in time

Let me take you on a journey back to 2001. 'Here she comes, glass half empty...'

That was my boss, in my early 20's. I was a very cynical person, and I worked as a claim's handler in an insurance company. I was working with high-profile, multinational clients and their customers. I was a technically excellent negotiator and a technical trainer, achieving the best results, but I lacked belief in myself and trust in others.

I had friends but I never ever mixed business with pleasure. I would go to lunch with some of my colleagues and I enjoyed their company but only for short periods because inside I couldn't see why they would want to spend time with me, 'what if we ran out of things to talk about?'

There was one colleague who I developed a great friendship with and back in those days we would extend our lunch chats whilst we put away our files and pulled our work for the next day. She would talk about plans with her Fiancé and one day she handed me an envelope.

I didn't much like opening things, gifts or otherwise, in front of people and so I thanked her and put it in my pocket.

May I ask you a question?

Have you ever not wanted to show up but also not wanted to not show up?

Have you ever been so crippled with fear that you simply couldn't show up?

That envelope contained a wedding invite. I hadn't been invited to a wedding before, and I didn't know what was expected of me. I verbally acknowledged the invite (I think) but when it came to the evening of the event, I got ready and found myself absolutely overcome with anxiety. I can see myself now, slumped, looking into my dressing table mirror. Listening to some horrible thoughts in my own mind... The time passing 'Tick Tock, Tick Tock', 'My god you are so stupid... you are late now...'

My eyes pricked, and within moments my makeup was spoiled and the outfit I was wearing had black smudged drips down the front. 'I couldn't go now… what a horrible friend I am.'

That night, I didn't show up. When the Bride returned from her honeymoon my absence wasn't discussed, and I felt heavy with guilt and regret at missing the 'Big Day' that she had been speaking to me about for months. That guilt still sits with me now.

New beginnings

Fast forward to 2015, I had separated from my children's dad. A friend I had met had told me I should become a coach and initially I didn't know what that meant. I responded with 'Er…. Thanks for the compliment, I do go to the gym, but I don't think I could be a personal trainer'. He explained he meant Life or Business Coaching, leadership training, and mindset work. He knew I loved helping others to explore ideas and see the great in themselves and I had a really good grasp on business from the multitude of financial services functions I had worked in. Having done a lot of work on myself, my outlook on life had changed dramatically and his thoughts planted a seed in my mind. 'What was this coaching thing? Could I be any good at it?'

At the end of 2015, after several months of sofa surfing, whilst the kid's dad stayed at the family home every other weekend, he got a flat. Friends and family had been very accommodating over the months preceding and whilst I felt out of place and a burden, I had largely enjoyed my time socialising, something I had given up unless it was with the children and parents of their friends. In January 2016 I started the year facing my first weekend alone in the house as the children went to stay with their dad in his new place. By this time my daughter was 10, my son 7 and, aside from a couple of nights off and going to work, I had never been away from them. As it was January, all of my friends were cutting back after the Christmas indulgence and so I was going to be in the house... alone. Quite honestly, the pain of knowing I was going to be without them was intense. I had no idea what I was going to do with myself and inside I was in a panic. I could imagine myself Bridget Jones style rocking in a corner and wailing, surrounded by empty wine bottles until they returned home. When the Christmas and New Year festivities were over all I could think about was the despair I was about to face for 3 whole days and nights as they were staying Thursday to Sunday. 'What was I going to do?!'

The turning point

On the Thursday, a Facebook advert popped up for a free 2-day coaching course in London. In all honesty I thought 'Oh, that will fill my time'. The idea petrified me but what was the alternative? Whilst I had excelled in my work, held meetings with senior leaders, delivered training and presented to multinational clients, that was really always for someone else and because somebody else had recognised something in me (I guess reflecting now, this was too). I felt extreme anxiety but nothing compared to the pain of being without my children and so I signed up. I remember telling a friend about it and her being baffled by my fear but for me, it was terrifying.

I caught a busy train early Saturday morning. When I finally found the venue, I looked up at the building. I became aware that my breathing was fast and shallow, and my thoughts were racing. I'd spent money I didn't have on a train ticket but, with the idea of an empty house at home, I thought 'Caroline you can't back out now!'.

I straightened my posture, went into the building, and was ushered through to a desk with queues of people signing in. I could just about see through the partition doors to a huge room beyond with hundreds of people choosing where to sit. I put pen to paper and wrote my name and then turned and bolted to the Ladies where I sat in a cubicle for what felt like forever. There were so many people in there it felt overwhelming. Head in my hands, my inner voice screaming 'What on earth were you thinking?' I straightened myself again, still in the safety of the loo, this helped to slow my breathing (I didn't know this to be a real technique at this point). I could hear my mum's voice in my mind, 'Head up, shoulders back, 3 smiles'. I washed my hands, straightened my posture even further in the mirror and headed towards the main room to find a seat.

The coaching course was a massive eye-opener. It wasn't the right training company for me, but I am hugely grateful for the part it played in the next leg of my journey. You see, I realised that I knew some of this 'coaching' stuff from my roles in financial services. I had attended courses and used professional goal setting at work and my time as a network marketer had helped me begin to change my mindset in positive ways. I met a new connection on this coaching course and in April 2016 we attended another course together, this time in Covent Garden, near to where my working life first began. The journey there was still tremendously scary but easier, I knew the area, I had someone to go with and the group was much smaller, around 20 people. I showed up!

As I reflect now, I realise that it felt safe, something I hadn't always felt in my working environment. The concepts that were shared in this course went way beyond goal setting. It might sound odd to you reading now but just that one day had a profound effect on me. I realised I wasn't really as stuck as I thought. I had choices. I felt lighter and more optimistic about the future. At this moment I didn't know how, but I knew I needed to learn more. I didn't really understand what this all was but realised 'people needed this... I needed this.' A few months later I signed up for an 8-month coaching course. This one course began to teach me the skills that were missing from my career. I felt so connected in this space and I really couldn't indulge myself enough. I was developing empowering techniques to help people realise the potential they have inside and in doing so my self-belief increased beyond measure. 'What a gift to be able to offer.'

I was invited to learn Neuro Linguistic Programming 6 months later. I had no clue what it was other than a 7-day intensive course in Marbella. In all honesty, I thought that the biggest things I would learn was getting on a plane by myself, working with strangers and trusting enough to be away from my children in another country for 8 whole days this time.

No one could have explained to me what becoming an NLP Practitioner would give me both personally and professionally. It absolutely transformed my communication skills and my perception of what we are capable of as humans. I knew I needed to bring this to more people ...

About a week after I returned from my trip, I returned to my desk after lunch and there was a little box on my desk, a gift from a friend. When I opened it, I burst into tears. I was no longer glass half empty. Inside the little box was a pen, on it read...

Caroline, Positive and Passionate!

In April 2017, a friend of a friend was selling a ticket to attend Tony Robbins' UPW event. I had been binge-watching Tony's videos for weeks at this point but had no clue that he ran events in the UK. In January, I had set myself a goal to build up a savings pot of cash and the pot just happened to cover the cost of the ticket and expenses. After freaking out somewhat about going with strangers and staying in a shared Airbnb, I bought the ticket! Tony's trainings are a combination of a rave and a seminar and, whilst I wanted to go, I was absolutely terrified again. This took all of the funds I had but I showed up! I became a fire walker for the first time, stomping across hot coals with 10,000 others at the Royal Victoria Dock alongside the Thames. Firewalking really does help you to realise that the seemingly impossible is absolutely possible. As humans we are capable of incredible things!

In October 2019, I was offered the chance to become an NLP Master Practitioner. This would be 2 weeks of intensive training, living with fellow students, retreat style, in the middle of nowhere in Portugal. The idea of being in a farmhouse in the middle of nowhere, in a foreign country, not even a shop in easy reach was petrifying. Still... I embraced the next level. I showed up!

In October 2020, when the world was still rather crazy, I put my hand up for redundancy, even I thought I was crazy! I left the safety net of the company that I had grown up with to show up more fully for my passions. In May 2021, my NLP Trainers training began. This was my chance to finally qualify to teach what I had been learning for 5 years!

I had become very ill in the last weeks of employment,

which is a different story that you may hear another time. I was still resting for a large part of most days and short of breath just standing. I can remember the speaker training and feeling dizzy with some of the breathing exercises. We had weeks of intense training and study when some days I couldn't hold myself together, my body was weak, and the bar was so high! Some days I had tears and some days I had smiles… every day, I showed up!

In December 2021 I was invited to speak at a big women's event in London. Armed with my heels, I shared my story that I wrote about in 'Determined to Rise' and I showed up. The event was pivotal for me in rejoining the dots to my 11-year-old entrepreneur self.

Skipping forward to March 2022, when I was volunteering at an awards evening for the Chartered Insurance Institute, there was another pivotal event where I was flabbergasted to be invited to become Deputy President of the Chelmsford and South Essex CII. This meant I would be President the following year and chair a council of over 20 members to serve a membership of more than 4,000 financial services professionals. I said 'Yes' and I committed to showing up!

I am not one to take on a role lightly and the following 24

months were a rollercoaster. Even though I was a volunteer, I made it my mission to understand as much about the CII/PFS and wider profession that I possibly could so that I could serve our membership in the best way during my tenure. I truly gave it my all and worked tirelessly into the evenings and weekends and whilst I am no longer President, I am still heavily involved and continue to do so.

I am truly grateful for my CII colleagues and wider network because they have also recognised and helped me to share my message even wider. I have earned the right to work with the most wonderful professionals, who share my ethics and values, which has blessed me with further opportunities to travel and deliver workshops, keynotes and trainings.

It has also been the most glamorous and difficult time of my professional career. Stage work and meetings by day and prestigious dinners by night, while both working to progress to NLP Master Trainer and starting my first solo coaching and NLP Practitioner programs in financial services. I took on a tremendous amount whilst also balancing some extremely personal and family challenges. I am proud to say that when I commit myself, by hook or by crook, I always show up!

Showing up and delivering has become my superpower and this part of my story has been previously delivered as a keynote speech and so it felt like the obvious thing to write about for this chapter. It truly has been a journey of Grit and Grace. I can tell you now that I do not find it easy, and my family see the other side very regularly. I really have developed an unwavering skill of quietening my doubts, leaving my troubles at the door no matter what, to do what I have told others that I will do.

Until I couldn't!

In early November, on an accountability session writing this very book chapter, I proudly messaged Tracey to say I was almost done. I had been in a completely hyper-focused state for over an hour. I closed the laptop, collected my thoughts and then it happened. I couldn't feel my right arm. I gave myself a wiggle and tried to stand, at which point, I realised I couldn't feel my right leg either and I collapsed back into the chair. Tears pricked in my eyes as I realised that my whole right side was numb.

I dismissed what was happening and began knocking my right leg to revitalise its mobility. I often become numb if I am fixed in one position, that was nothing unusual for me but not to this extent. More than 30 minutes passed with little improvement. I reopened the laptop and searched. My inner voice was telling me that I shouldn't believe what I was reading. 'Google always dramatizes symptoms.' I continued to physically shake myself until the feeling returned. I told myself that I was being silly and went to bed. 'I was probably just tired and sat funny whilst in hyperfocus. Tomorrow will be a new day.'

The following day I was aware of a weakness and felt absolutely exhausted doing the smallest of things. I was conscious that I had had a particularly stressful month or so. I plodded on with the days tasks but taking it easy.

On the Friday I had already arranged what I considered 'self-care.' This was in the form of Osteopathic treatment for my back followed by showing up in the evening for a friend's product business launch. When I arrived for my Osteopathic treatment, I explained what happened earlier in the week and was urged to go to see the Doctor, 'just to be sure.' A bit shocked and very emotional, I drove straight there. I had a call from my GP 5 minutes later and was asked to come back to the surgery at 6 pm before they closed.

When I arrived, my blood pressure was taken. Lights were shone in my eyes and throat, I think. Various limbs knocked with a little hammer, and I was asked to squeeze with my hands and push with my legs and then asked to walk in a straight line. (Like the old days test for alcohol, a bit before my time but I've seen it in old movies – haha). After the assessments, I sat back in the chair. The Doctor thanked me for engaging in the tests and then held my hands.

I will never forget that moment. She asked me if I had looked in the mirror to which I said 'No'. She suggested I didn't. She then said she needed to do the tests to confirm what she had observed when we walked down the corridor to her office. She asked me if I was aware that I was dragging my right leg. I wasn't. Again, I felt my eyes prick with tears.

'My dear, do you have anyone with you?'

'Yes, my partner is in the waiting room.'

'My dear, I think you may have had a stroke. You need to go to A&E straight away.'

'What was I hearing?' My first thought being, 'I can't possibly. My friend's business launch is important. I have to show up!'

Reflections

Today is the Anniversary of one of my best friends passing last year and I am sat in a hospital café, following yet another scan. My symptoms and ongoing mild weakness currently have no explanation despite having every test available. This frustrated me for a while as I have been searching for a message amongst the drama and the analyst in me is craving data to work with to improve my health. Whilst I am left feeling very confused, I also feel blessed.

Abby, I am glad I got to show up for you in your last few days and for the encouragement you gave me to push through my fears and continue to do so. You showed me that life is so short and precious but whilst my brain heard that message in logical terms, I failed to really get it until now.

I am one of the lucky ones.

I am grateful to have been fast-tracked with dozens of tests and scans that some wait months or even years for. Many also never get the tests they need.

I am grateful that my diary happened to have space to show up to literally dozens of hours of medical appointments.

I am grateful to have still been able to show up to every single other commitment that I had made.

So, for those that heard my keynote last year… the message has changed just a little and I believe in a good way.

Life is a gift and each day we have the blessing of being able to show up for ourselves and for the things and people that are important to us. This period has helped me to review what I will be showing up for in my next chapter of life.

Mentors (official or unofficial) are on our path to help us move more quickly through things that caused them pain. Coaches are there to help you explore your options, and what is right for you, to challenge your thinking, and help you to make decisions.

I never thought that I had choices. I thought I had chosen my path and therefore that was the way life was going to be. The good, the bad, and the ugly. Life before my professional coaching and NLP journey was happening to me and I felt completely out of control. Hear me now, I still feel that way sometimes and the last few months have reminded me of that.

I believe that every challenge that I have is because it is my calling to become a better human to enable more people to be more, do more and achieve more in an aligned way as you navigate this world with Grit and Grace. Authentically, Ethically and Successfully. That's why I am sharing this message.

So, grab a notebook and let me ask you this…

- If you were to review all aspects and live your best life what would that be like? (Explore for example your, Career, Health, Relationships, Finances, Home Environment, Charity/helping others, Fun, Personal Growth). Dream Big!
- What are you currently showing up for? Are all of these things aligned to where you want to be?

- What are you currently not showing up for that is important to you?
- What will happen if you choose to show up for more of those important things?
- What will happen if you don't show up for more of those important things?
- What won't happen if you don't show up for more of those important things?
- What won't happen if you do show up for more of those important things?
- What if you could choose to change and stop doing some of those things that are not serving you?
- What can you be grateful for?
- Is there anything you are going to commit to doing as a result of your reflections?

Thank you for listening to this part of my journey and gifting me the time of your presence.

I would like to return the gift and offer you some of my time to explore any questions you have or even share your story.

Follow the link to find my diary and let me help you and/or your team become the best that you can be.

SCAN ME

SCAN ME

SCAN ME

Website: www.enablingwings.com/Discovery

LinkedIn: www.linkedin.com/in/enablingwings

Email: carolinemartin@enablingwings.com

Other Book Collaborations

Determined to Rise with Queens in Business

Courage with Sarah Makinde

Caroline is also writing a solo book in 2025. Email for more information or to be put on the waiting list for details!

"YOU CAN HAVE A GOOD DAY OR A
BAD DAY. WHICH DO YOU CHOOSE?"

Caroline Martin

GRIT AND GRACE

CHAPTER 3
BY DANI MEIGHEN

The Girl Before the Grit

I had, what a lot of people would probably describe as a perfect childhood. My parents were the greatest team, they supported me every single day of my life and were always there to catch me when I fell. It was a home full of love, and everything they did, they did for me and my future. Looking back, it felt a bit like they'd wrapped a soft blanket of safety around me, and I never needed to worry about anything.

Despite this though, I always struggled with a huge lack of confidence and lack of self-worth. I doubted myself regularly, and always just tried to blend in with the background, hoping no one would notice me. I never had a huge friendship circle, I was definitely never one of the 'popular' kids, and always wondered where I fit in.

When I was around six years old, my parents booked me in to start dancing lessons locally. I guess they saw my lack of confidence too and thought this may be an avenue to build on that. It started off just as an activity, something I attended weekly, something for me outside of school, and although I enjoyed it, I still, even at that age, had that feeling of not being like the others. They all had their friendship groups, they all knew each other, and they all just seemed to belong.

Looking back, I realise it was just my lack of confidence holding me back to just go up to those groups, to start chatting, and to become friends with them, but I guess this is what we learn as we get older.

Over time, although still that shy little girl, dancing started to become my sanctuary. I'd still go into class and keep myself to myself but when the music started, it just felt like a switch had been flipped, and I just felt a huge rush of excitement and happiness, like I could finally be me and not have to focus on my insecurities. It became a place to switch off from the outside world.

Dancing to me, wasn't about having perfect steps but about teaching me lessons I probably didn't even realise I needed at the time. Like the importance of showing up, even if you don't quite feel like it, ESPECIALLY when you don't feel like it, because you can guarantee that no matter how down I may have felt, or how out of place I felt, that when I stepped into that class and started dancing, all was good with the world again. My childhood taught me the power of unconditional love and support, but my dancing, slowly but surely taught me the power of believing in myself, as I went onto perform on stage, fly through exams, and eventually go on to complete a degree in dance and perform as a career.

For years, I went through life slowly building on that confidence, and with the unconditional hope that things would always work out for the best one way or another, but as life took it's turns and I grew older, I realised that safety net I'd always had and counted on wasn't guaranteed. That's when I really started to understand the meaning of resilience – not something we're born with, but something we build over time.

A Moment that Changed Everything

The 15th of June 2020 is a day I will never forget! The moment I heard the words no one ever wants to hear. "You have breast cancer." It was honestly like you hear people talk about when they say the world literally stopped, everything I'd ever done flashed before me, and I just knew in that instant that life was never going to be the same.

Not only did I have two young children, the youngest just six months old, we'd also recently gone into lockdown in the March, and now I was looking head-on at a rigorous regime of treatment which would more than likely wipe me out and take away the plans I had with my boys whilst on maternity leave.

All the questions started flooding my head 'Have I caused this?' 'What will my boys do without me?' 'Should I have spotted it sooner?' I wasn't only facing an awful illness but my own mortality.

Before we go any further, bit of a backstory about how I found the cancer and the importance of getting second opinions. I'd literally been lying on the bed one day and my eldest came in and gave me a cuddle. As he got up my hand brushed past my breast and instantly, I felt something, I just knew it wasn't right! I called the doctor immediately who saw me that day and instantly put me at ease by telling me 'As you're breastfeeding, it's more than likely just a blocked milk duct but we'll send you for a scan just to make sure as that's procedure.' I saw a consultant who repeated the same thing so by this point I felt confident all was fine, until the moment they sent me for an ultrasound. You know that feeling when the atmosphere just seems to change? He looked at me and said I'm just going to take a biopsy too and send you for a mammogram. I just knew! Long story short, on June 15th, 2020, they sat me down, walked me into a room with Breast Cancer nurses sat in the corner and said those words.

I very quickly started an intense treatment of chemo and started to lose my hair, which strangely was one of the things I worried about the most, which to some may sound so vain, but apparently quite a common feeling. I think as women, it's a part of us, a part of our identity, and it was just fading away slowly, day by day. The cumulative effect of the chemo was taking hold, and I was feeling weaker, the sickness was unbearable, and I was spending less and less time with the children as I was too poorly in bed.

This however, made me start to see things with a different

outlook, like a sharper lens had been put on life, and that those moments which I'd once taken for granted, time with loved ones, moments of joy became my anchors and kept me going. I realised that before this, I'd just been running on autopilot, plodding through life as if nothing could harm us.

Months passed and I endured more chemo, followed by surgery, radiotherapy, and yet more chemo. It was just the gift that kept on giving, but eventually, in May 2021 I rang that bell! My treatment was over, and in some ways that was the hardest part because people just think you're all cured and back to normal but actually your life has just been turned upside down, everything you once thought has disappeared, and the constant worry is always there in the back of your head, so no, things are not 'back to normal.'

What I knew though was that I was not going to go back to 'plodding.' To doing things that didn't serve me, and that was when I made the decision to leave the security of my 9-5 job, and step into the unknown. I wanted to work to live, not live to work so I started my own business. It was terrifying but compared to what I had just faced, the only choice for me to make.

Looking back, my diagnosis was one of the hardest chapters of my life, but it was also what taught me about strength, courage and the importance of living with intention. It set me on a path to not just rebuild, but to thrive.

Building a Life on My Own Terms

It was time to enter the world of Entrepreneurship. Knowing I had to step away from the 9-5 and start my own business was daunting but absolutely felt like the right choice, and an opportunity arose to join a long-standing franchise business as a franchisee in my local area. With my background in dance and early years, the diddi dance franchise was perfect. Teaching preschool-age children to dance in a fun and relaxed environment, creating a space where children could build confidence through movement and dance just as I had as a child. Not only did I get to do something I loved, but I also had the backup of an already existing and proven model, which would ease me into the world of business without feeling completely alone. I finally had the opportunity to create something of my own which I could be proud of and make a real difference to local children and families.

However, the transition into self-employment wasn't without its challenges, I had to learn how to juggle it all, marketing, finances, systems, all whilst still being present for my family, and trying to pursue that work life balance which I had craved.

A year down the line, and I finally felt like I was getting in the swing of things. I was building up a steady and loyal customer base, I was really enjoying the marketing side and social media side of things. People were even asking me to help with their social media marketing as I'd made it look so easy.

That's when I started thinking, who says I can only have one business? Maybe I could explore other avenues too. Over the following year I worked closely with a business growth group for budding Entrepreneurs, as although I knew I'd like to try my hand at something else, I didn't know what I could feasibly do, or if I had the appropriate skills.

During this time I learnt so much and achieved things I never would have even imagined. The first venture being creating and publishing 3 children's Spanish books. I absolutely loved languages as a kid and had gone on to pursue them at a higher level, and lived in Spain for a three-year period following my time at uni where I picked it up too, so I had the idea to combine my love of languages and early years to create these books, which were published and sold on Amazon! Who even was I?! Normal people don't do things like this, do they?

Working alongside a group of people who believed in me, who supported me and who guided me in the right direction was everything, and I know I wouldn't have achieved half of what I have without them. This led me to pursue other businesses, from selling products on Etsy, Social Media management and running a business membership for Mums.

Each and every one of these businesses taught me something. They reinforced the importance of resilience, of adaptability, of knowing that sometimes it's ok to have gone down the wrong path. At least you've given it a try and now know it's maybe not for you but something else is. They showed me the importance of really staying true to my purpose!

This is something which over the following year, I really needed to keep telling myself. I had got through the cancer treatment, I had this new lease of life, I was so proud of what I'd achieved but running alongside that, my marriage was breaking down. By September 2023, after almost 16 years, it ended, and life was going to have to continue on a completely different path than I had planned!

Following this separation, one thing became really clear, my journey wasn't just about building businesses anymore, it was about building myself. There were many times when I thought to myself 'Why am I doing this?' Life was feeling pretty tough, and often that little nagging voice of 'Why is everything happening to me?' kept creeping in.

However, the more I worked on myself, and focussed on the positives...I had beaten cancer, I had started my own successful business, I had two wonderful, well-rounded children and the most amazing friends and family I could wish for. Why would I let this time of difficulty push all that to the side? Instead, it was time to use all those difficulties, all those setbacks and challenges to keep pushing me forward. I've done it before, and I can do it again I told myself!

I was already working with business Mums within my membership, and I started noticing a common thread - they were often feeling overwhelmed, stretched too thin, and struggling to find their footing, and from my own experience, realised that sometimes these big life changes leave us feeling a little lost, and like our identity has gone in some way. Whether that be illness, divorce, or parenthood, everyone has their own struggles which can really impact how they see or feel about themselves.

That's when I realised, I needed to shift my focus, not just to Mums in business but to Mums & women in general, and to use my personal experiences, my struggles, my challenges to really help them navigate life's storms with strength, confidence and resilience!

Turning Struggles into Strength

I remember sat on my sofa New Years Eve 2023, the kids had gone to bed, and I just broke! I just sat there in pieces whilst the tears just kept coming. It was like everything I'd been holding in just came flooding out. My marriage had ended, I needed to find us a new home, and still had to make sure my businesses were running, which was now even more imperative.

Facing my own life's challenges head-on has shaped me into someone who no longer sees obstacles as barriers but as opportunities to grow. I've learned the resilience isn't just about getting on with things, it's about adapting and learning from a situation, and finding a strength from vulnerability.

It was not long after this that I had that moment of clarity, I could really help people through sharing my own struggles. I made the decision to pivot my business, and work with women who have gone through their own struggles, and who now are maybe at a crossroads, have lost their identity, and are suffering with a lack of confidence or drive. I wanted to show women that no matter what we go through, we can use it to push us forward. One of my favourite sayings is *'Our setbacks are setups for a comeback,'* and I absolutely believe this. It would have been so easy for me to dwell on the fact I'd been dealt the 'cancer' card, or think because my marriage ended that 'I'm just not good enough,' but where would that have got me?

Instead, I used these setbacks to make things better both for me and other women out there who may not have the support or the mindset to know how to push forward yet.

What I didn't anticipate was how much my story would resonate with others.

One client said, *'Having support from someone who just 'gets' it is so important.'*

Another one said, *'I always come away feeling much more positive and less stressed after speaking to Dani.'*

I didn't become this person overnight, and what I speak to my clients about and support them with are also things I work on myself personally. I still suffer with imposter syndrome, with not feeling good enough, with lack of confidence, it's natural. The difference is I now use strategies to push past those feelings and remember what is important, why I'm doing what I do and how it can genuinely help others.

Rebuilding confidence isn't about perfection—it's about progress. One exercise I love is asking women to list three things they're proud of each day. These don't have to be huge accomplishments; one woman I worked with felt proud simply for making it through the day with a smile. It's the little wins that remind us of our strength.

I also encourage people to create what I call a 'Confidence Toolbox.' Mine started with a playlist of empowering songs I'd blast on days when I didn't feel like showing up for myself. Now, I suggest adding other tools: a list of affirmations, a photo that makes you smile, or even a scented candle that reminds you to breathe or brings back happy memories.

If you're looking for a place to start, try this: tonight, take a quiet moment to write one thing you like about yourself or something you did well today. Even if it feels hard, keep going. Confidence is built one small step at a time.

Now I'm at a point where I feel really aligned with what I am doing and where I am headed. I still love every second of my dance business which is still going strong and growing bigger and better, but alongside this, knowing that I am making a difference and using my difficult times for something good makes me feel super proud of myself, and of all the women I work with too.

I have big plans for the future, and my next goal with the business would be to have a big in person event where we all get together, listen to some amazing inspirational guest speakers, hear each other's journeys, and really build each other up. There is nothing quite like a group of strong, inspirational women being in a room together and really taking steps to grow, learn and thrive.

Find your Strength, Rewrite your Story

Life has a way of throwing challenges our way—whether it's illness, divorce, the ups and downs of parenthood, or just that feeling of being stuck and unsure of what's next. If any of this resonates with you, I want you to know you're not alone. My Facebook group is a safe, supportive space for women just like you—women who've been through it, who are finding their way, and who are ready to rebuild their confidence and take the next step, whatever that might look like.

If you're ready to start making small but meaningful changes, check out my Linktree for free resources, ways to connect with me, and opportunities to work together. Whether it's through a conversation, a coaching session, or just sharing your story in the group, I'd love to help you find your strength again and remind you that you're capable of so much more than you realise.

Don't wait to make the life you want happen, let's do it now TOGETHER!

Facebook Group:
www.facebook.com/MumsAchievingMore

Linktree: linktr.ee/MumsAchievingMore

TikTok: www.tiktok.com/@dani_mumsachievingmore

"THE HARDEST CHAPTERS OF YOUR
LIFE CAN BECOME THE MOST
POWERFUL PARTS OF YOUR STORY."

Dani Neighen

GRIT AND GRACE

CHAPTER 4

BY GEMMA LUXTON

From Front Line to Front Bottom

At school I dreamt of being a doctor, but my grades didn't reflect my ambition. No matter how hard I worked and how much I knew, I seemed unable to show that in exams. The careers adviser suggested I be a carer, which really did not feel right. I was the class clown, larger than life, to mask my disappointment at being in the bottom sets, and not feeling like I fitted in. What I did not realise until decades later was that by adopting the FAIL (First Attempt at Learning) philosophy, I was able to see my failures as attempts and keep trying. Eventually, I went from poor GCSE results to diplomas, a degree and now running my own business. When we find our unique superpowers, life becomes easier, and when we look at failure as a first attempt at learning, opportunities are endless.

Growing up in a garrison town, my options were limited, particularly because exams were my nemesis. Time would start, my brain would freeze, and the paper might as well have been in Swahili. It wasn't that I didn't know the material; I just couldn't translate it onto paper. Talk to me, and I'd explain it all, but the second an exam rolled around, I'd fall apart. So, I made peace with the fact that I'd never be a doctor, but aiming for a "carer" did not seem encouraging either. I looked for an alternative pathway.

• Marry a soldier. Nope, not for me.

• Go to university. Unlikely with my GCSE results.

• Join the Army or RAF. Hmm... sleeping in a field didn't appeal, so the RAF won by process of elimination. I still felt a calling to go into a medical role, so I looked at being a medic.

Teachers and school friends told me I wouldn't ever get into the RAF and couldn't hack it, so off I went to prove them wrong(ish).

Cleaner to the stars

Nothing about my journey was straightforward. I couldn't join immediately; medics weren't being recruited, and I needed to lose weight. Driven by determination, the desire to prove people wrong, and naivety, I did what any 17-year-old would do: I turned to a very questionable fitness regime. Eating nothing but jacket potato and beans and doing infamous "bin bag runs." If you've never heard of it, you wear a bin bag under your clothes whilst running, sweating buckets, topped off with a sauna because someone swore it worked. (For the record: it doesn't, it's not safe, I was just lucky.)

Always a worker, my drive and determination really kicked in. Whilst waiting to join up, and to save for a car, well to pay for the insurance which was more than the car cost, I did a bit of everything. Lifeguarding; working in the chip shop; the pub; a mess hand on the Army base, and I even worked as a chambermaid, maybe I should add "Cleaner to the stars" to my resume after cleaning Pauline Quirk's room!

I firmly believed that nothing is beneath me when it comes to work. This mindset came from my mother, she used to tell us the cleaner is just as important as the CEO. Throughout my career and as a parent I believe in treating everyone as equal and never ask someone to do something that you wouldn't do yourself. Of course, you don't have to do the jobs you don't want to; you can always choose to have others do them for you, but you have to:

a. Be able to do the job should you need to

b. Remember that the person is just as important as you, - they are more important if they are doing a job, you do not want to do, always respect them and treat them fairly.

Passing Out

Despite the ridiculous physical training routine, miraculously I passed everything, and just shy of my 18th birthday, my mum signed the paperwork handing me over to the Military's care. (because I was under 18, they technically became my legal guardians, the RAF owned me!)

How much faith did people have in me? The general consensus was "give her two weeks" before I'd crumble into failure. "Empowering, valued and supported," I think not!

My new guardian gave me ample opportunities to meet that 2-week deadline and throw in the towel, including a unique 18th birthday gift—a story for another book, but let's just say it involved an unforgettable introduction to tear gas.

2 Weeks

Basic training was brutal. I polished shoes, perfected bed packs, and polished floors only to strip them again for no logical reason. It was a nightmare, I have never been good at taking orders, but I made it through, and looking back, it shaped me and prepared me in so many ways.

Spoiler alert: I lasted the two weeks and 1,149 more! I completed a full 22 years of service, travelled the world, deployed to conflicts and advanced through the ranks. I worked in amazing and humbling positions; saw places I never knew existed and met people I never thought I would— Ross Kemp in Afghanistan and tea at Kensington Palace!

Academic Struggles and Dyslexia Diagnosis

I still failed every exam I took the first time around and struggled with academia (I didn't even know what that meant) but was good hands-on and explaining. Not that this mattered, everything was graded and you had to pass the grade. Whilst working in a pharmacy and loving my job, I went on a course to fly with patients, but I failed the final exam. I had flashbacks to school and failing, but one nurse wondered if I was dyslexic. She fought to help me and tested me orally (asking me questions, not a dental examination), and I passed with 100%. Despite her efforts, without an official diagnosis, I was failed and sent back to my unit. This was seen as a disgrace and massive disrespect for the unit, life changed that day.

My independence was removed, and I was removed from the job I loved despite not making a mistake or causing any harm to a patient, because of a written exam (ironically my error rates were less than my peers because I did additional checks). Supported much?! The confidence I had grown over the years was ripped away; I reverted back to my never-achieve attitude. It was easier to stop trying than be publicly known as a failure. This, however, was my introduction to First Attempt In Learning (F.A.I.L.ing), I was assessed, my dyslexia was officially diagnosed, it's probably the first test I passed with flying colours!

People's attitudes changed, they started to recognise my ability and allowed me to do things differently— Life changing, a massive weight was lifted, and I embraced this.

Personal Growth and Education

So what? I became unstoppable, becoming a doctor was a stretch, but I was determined to get as educated and qualified as I could and I was happy to F.A.I.L. With the support of good line managers, and life lessons on how not to do it from a few, I became a mentor and coach to many peers and superiors. I found a love for education I had never known and set out to get qualified.

F.A.I.L number 1: - an Open University Law Degree. Why? Because someone told me I couldn't! I completed 2 yrs before realising I didn't want to do it and was only doing it to prove I could. I chose then to stop and start focusing on things that served me and my future visions (except the bus licence, that's for another story!)

I qualified and specialized in Aeromedical evacuation (the course I initially failed) and I spent 20 yrs doing this.

I got back in the pharmacy, gained Diplomas in Practice Management and Pharmaceutical Sciences, became the Lead Human Factors facilitator for the entire Defence Medical Academy; completed coaching and mentoring courses, specialised in Leadership, Management and healthcare.

I still failed, but I embraced the F.A.I.L. and eventually achieved a BSc (Hon) degree.

I would work up to the last minute, fail and have to resubmit assignments, (I didn't pass any first time), there were many times I thought about giving up, especially when I deleted my whole assignment at 0155am with a deadline of 0200am, but I kept going, I wanted to prove I could and I did. Some people would be embarrassed by a 3rd class degree, not me! This wasn't just a piece of paper; it was testament to resilience, determination and proving people wrong.

My degree was via distance learning whilst working full-time, teaching and mentoring the next generation of medics across the Services, adapting and created new teaching materials: completing assignments and undertaking frontline ambulance shifts as I trained to become an Associate Ambulance Practitioner (AAP); job role changes, family health issues, during the chaos of the COVID-19 pandemic (2020-2022). I also homeschooled my five-year-old twins - not traditionally. By six, my daughter was proficient at taking blood and could confidently explain more about emergency medicine than most teenagers - leading to an awkward moment where she (rightly) corrected hospital staff on their techniques whilst impressing them with her knowledge. Her dream? To become a doctor.

In true form, the day I graduated was a challenge, arriving late, I got changed in a car park and we had to get straight home to our son who didn't attend. Crossed that stage, with my wife and daughter cheering in the audience, wearing a gown over my uniform, my medals on my chest and a cap on my head it felt surreal, proving that resilience pays off, it was a celebration of every sleepless night, every F.A.I.L, every challenge, every achievement. That day wasn't just about a degree it was a day even I didn't really believe would happen and my biggest "You Can't" achieved.

Life Changes and Career Transition

Life was good; married to my best friend, two beautiful (cheeky) children, a loving dog, a stable well-paid job and suddenly that security was ripped away with one email titled: "TERMINATION OF SERVICE."

I did know my 22 years contract was coming to an end (they call it natural wastage) however;

1. An email entitled "termination" was brutal, and unexpected

2. I had convinced myself that it was just an admin process, and that the RAF would see my value in the next 13 months and offer me an extension of service.

I used the resettlement time and money to upskill and qualify within the NHS, I saw these as extensions of my qualifications, someone called me a" qualification whore" and I swelled with pride, the girl with no academic hope was now rolling in qualifications!

New Business Venture

Whilst training I discovered natural treatments to rejuvenate skin and help people feel younger. Mind blown, I researched, trained and started practicing on friends and family.

"Can you fix my fanny?" Yep, you read that right. I nearly spat out my coffee! My friend had watched a program about non-surgical vaginal rejuvenation and wanted my help. This was the first I had heard of it; so I started researching, having suffered from urinary incontinence since a young age, I knew how debilitating it was, so as soon as I found life-changing benefits after just one session I was invested and looking for courses.

Why not? The RAF gave me resettlement money so why not spend it and change lives? Full transparency, the 15-year-old rebel in me also thought it would be amusing for the high-ranking officers to have to sign off on a Vaginal rejuvenation course!

The Vagician is born!

The RejuvaLux business was born with a new pathway and

visions; helping women take back control of their lives, 100% naturally. Ridding the world of life-debilitating conditions; empowering and building confidence one woman at a time!

Fully trained—tick.

Equipment and insurance—tick.

Personal experience (I don't advocate something I hadn't tried)—tick.

I was ready to change the lives of all the women worrying about leaking when sneezing or coughing, who limit playtime with their children/grandchildren for fear of "accidents," who avoid intimacy because of pain or discomfort, who have become a shell of their former self and lack confidence.

RejuvaLux started as a tiny dream, one I wasn't even sure I could pull off. I didn't have a wealthy investor or a hidden inheritance. I had grit, determination, and an unwavering belief in what I was doing. My goal was simple: to help people feel their best naturally. Starting with my "fix my fanny" friend whose results were so spectacular she called me a "Vaginal Magician" and dubbed me "Gemma the Vagician."

The time for the RAF to extend my contract came and went (no offer of a new contract) and before I knew it I was a civilian, a veteran and a clueless business owner, living in a new area, with no clients and no idea of how to run a business! Cue a little (lot) of panic - the military perks, subsidised housing (taken directly from wages), free health and dental care, job security, sick/holiday pay, all gone. Now it was up to me to make money, and nothing was secure. No pressure! When I introduced the non-surgical vaginal rejuvenation, I knew I was stepping into unchartered territory. These weren't topics people openly discussed, but I saw the need. Women were struggling in silence, I was determined to give them a voice—and a solution, I knew that as soon as people knew about the natural treatments, they would want to know more.

F.A.I.L. I have a super niche product that people will want, but no one knows about it so I have to educate people on the benefits. Easy, just get a few people in, give away the treatment and get some reviews, right? NOPE

F.A.I.L – in our society women don't talk about issues "down there", getting someone to do a video or testimonial is very hard.

Now I am in a predicament: No one knows who I am, hardly anyone knows that the treatments even exist, Reality check "Gemma the Vagician" and "Fix my Fanny" friend shouting how good the treatment is doesn't reach the audience needed to change the world. So I headed on a social media journey and back to education to learn how to reach the right people.

I know very little about social media, having spent years avoiding it, so when I posted on Facebook and Instagram, I just assumed that was it, everyone would now know and I would be inundated with customers, changing the lives of millions of women who'd be knocking down my (virtual) door and we would live happily ever after. Spoiler - this is not how business works.

F.A.I.L - I quickly learned that getting clients isn't as simple as posting on social media platforms. There were days when

I doubted anyone was interested at all, questioning if I could succeed and wanting to throw in the towel, someone would tell me to give it up, that it was time to think about a safe job. Oh, don't tell me I can't do something so I would look for a new way to get my message out.

Speaking at events and on podcasts to educate as many people as I could. You don't know what you don't know, and I can honestly say there have only been 3 occasions where I have spoken in a group and there have been people who have heard of the treatments before that day.

That said, bills don't pay themselves so back to the good old days, long hours and hard work. I had to put my Ambulance training to good use and work other jobs, ironically including a job as a carer, so I suppose the assessment in school was eventually right! I trained in additional aesthetic treatments, some natural like the plasma fibroblast, and others using man-made products, but soon realized that I didn't have a passion for Botox or filler and quickly stopped, staying true to myself and my values and focusing on the natural self-healing route. Not every treatment works for every person, and I've had to have honest conversations with clients about their expectations. But I've always stood by my values: honesty, transparency, and a commitment to doing what's right—even if it's not the easy route. I met some brilliant people who supported and helped me but still I F.A.I.L a lot and that's the way I like it!

What keeps me going?

Messages from clients reminding me why I do this.

"You've changed my life."

"Guess what I did…"

"I don't know what you did to me, but it worked, I haven't worn a pad all day!"

"I had the best orgasm ever last night."

"I had sensation I haven't felt in 15 years."

And my absolute favourite from a partner who was worried about his wife, "thank you for giving me my wife back, her confidence is so much better and she is a better version of her old self."

The Future is as Big as I Want it to Be

Currently I am training and supporting a friend in setting up her own RejuvaLux, so a franchise is looking likely, and it has been suggested I venture into the corporate world to help CEOs and directors better understand and support employees. Not just female employees, but also the often forgotten men or same-sex partners who are the support and often the caregiver. I am grateful for my network for their support with innovative ideas.

Another book, I have enjoyed writing this but there is so much more so look out for the series of very fortunate events that have been my life coming to print.

Treatment on the NHS? I believe the vaginal treatment should be available to everyone via the NHS… watch this space.

Here's the thing: I'm not a multimillionaire (yet). I don't have a flashy car or a mansion (yet). I'm just a girl from a council estate who decided to follow the path of helping people. I am F.A.I.L. ing and I am achieving and only I decide what I can and cannot do (yet)

I am Gemma, "The Vagician" Luxton. Founder, CEO & Director of RejuvaLux BSc (Hons), BTEC (Pharmaceutical Science), DipAAP, DipAMSPAR (Practice Management), LCGI, AfCGI, Level 6 Women's Health, CERAD, LS&GC Medal, PSV License Ordained Deacon, Universal Life Church. Quite different from the "Gemma Lou" my mother just to call me at home but still me, the girl who still can't spell, who gets confused with words, and who people always underestimate.

I hope my story has inspired you, not because it's extraordinary but because it's real. "You're stronger than you think, and more capable than you know."

If you're ready to start your journey—whether it's taking control of your health, exploring new possibilities, or even joining the RejuvaLux franchise—I'd love to hear from you.

Website: www.rejuvalux.co.uk

LinkedIn: https://www.linkedin.com/in/gemma-luxton-the-vagician/

"YOU CAN'T F.A.I.L IF YOU DON'T TRY,
BUT IF YOU DON'T TRY YOU WILL
NEVER FLY."

Gemma, the Vagician

GRIT AND GRACE

CHAPTER 5

By JULIE BILBOE

Mary's Place® From loss to legacy: supporting tomorrow's new professionals

I am Julie Bilboe-Crane, a Nurse Lecturer and the proud mum of Mary-Lou, whose legacy inspired Mary's Place®.

I am the founder and CEO of Mary's Place®: a non-profit organisation which supports newly qualified professionals as they make the often-overwhelming transition from student to professional. We currently work with nurses, but our vision is to expand. The challenges we address in nursing exist in many professions. I will share more on this later. For now, let me tell you about Mary-Lou, my daughter, the inspiration behind Mary's Place®.

Mary-Lou

Mary-Lou Abbott was 22 years old when she died unexpectedly in January 2020 of meningio-encephalitis secondary to adenovirus. She was previously a fit and well MA Political Theory student who had graduated (LLB) from the University of Sheffield in July 2019. Mary-Lou was strong-minded but sensitive. She had excellent friends and a long-term boyfriend, Jason. Mary-Lou loved travelling and spent much of her undergraduate Year 3 visiting friends who were doing their Year Abroad. Lou (as I tended to call her) was sensible and dependable, with a listening ear and an eye for detail. She was also good fun and a brilliant storyteller. She had plans, and all who knew her felt sure she was going to make a difference in the world. Lou's death was a huge shock to everyone. She was unwell for just one week. I was on holiday in Lanzarote for most of that time. I remember having a horrible sense of mother's intuition about the situation. Hospital staff and family who were present with Lou tried to reassure me that she was OK.

Despite the reassurance, I had dark thoughts and uncomfortable feelings deep in the pit of my stomach. The flight home was horrendous. Being out of contact for so very long was excruciating. Lou was sedated, intubated and in Intensive Care when I got home. I did have a brief conversation with her. She knew I was there. We had hope. Devastatingly, the feeling of hope was short-lived. Lou died the next day. We spent a long time at the hospital after her death, it was Lou's wish to be an organ donor. The selfless act of organ donation gave some initial meaning to her loss and provided more comfort than one might imagine.

When we returned home from the hospital, I prepared myself for the practicality of going into Lou's bedroom. I knew that if I didn't do this immediately, it would become a huge barrier. When I stepped into Mary-Lou's bedroom, my eyes were drawn to a small purple box sitting by her bedside. A deck of Tarot cards. I remember standing there, confused, knowing that my life had just been irreversibly split into two: before Lou's death and after. With hindsight, those Tarot cards were the catalyst to the development of Mary's Place®. But at the time, I was just a mother trying to make sense of a world that no longer had her daughter in it. It was bizarre and a little bit scary if I am honest.

Weeks later, I learned the Tarot cards had been a gift from a university friend. At first, I left them untouched. But as time passed, curiosity took hold, and I found myself drawn to them. Strangely, they felt like a bridge to Mary-Lou, something of hers that I could still hold onto. In my search for healing, I explored every modality I could find: Reiki, Tarot, coaching, and more. Some might find it surprising, but for me, learning became healing. Each of these practices helped me navigate grief, and in turn, I began to see how they could support others.

The development of Mary's Place®

An early idea for Mary's Place® was that it would be a healing centre. A place for new holistic practitioners to gain experience in delivering healing services, under my watchful eye. As an experienced nurse and lecturer, I know what to look for when delivering a quality service. I also investigated the idea of Mary's Place® being a coaching enterprise. I was part of several coaching groups. All of which talked about the importance of having 'an audience' when developing a coaching business. By this point, I was an established Tarot reader (you can read more about that in the book: Women Who Win). As a Tarot reader, I read for (and coached) people from all walks of life and did not have a particular audience – nor did I want one. Whatever Mary's Place® was going to be, it needed to feel right and not forced.

Thankfully, I was in no rush to progress, these were just ideas. Distractions you might call them. The holistic business was a 'side hustle'. I still had my job at the university. At the time of Lou's death, I was at the start of a two-year secondment as Centre Manager for Liverpool Head and Neck Centre (LHNC). It was exciting and I could not have wished to work with a more supportive team as I tried to navigate my new (and largely unwanted) life. I gained experience in starting up new initiatives and I learned a lot about leadership. Without the nurturing, life-affirming experience of working with LHNC, I believe would not have had the energy to return to teaching. I now feel sure that the secondment opportunity was sent to me for a reason beyond the obvious.

I returned to teaching in November 2021. It took a while to settle back into my lecturing role. There were many low points, with lots of memories triggered. It was not easy. In September 2022, I was due to run a Year 3 'leadership module' with which I was very familiar. It was the first module I had led when I commenced at the university in 2005. I was comfortable with the material and did not pay too much attention to the planning. At the last minute, I had an epiphany:

"I can't teach this module the way I have always done it. I have changed; the world has changed. It is not right to not share the new things I have learned during my period of self-development."

With just days to spare, I rewrote the timetable, starting with the inclusion of self-leadership and self-awareness. The content still met the module's requirements. But the focus shifted, acknowledging the very real challenges that nurses were facing. Eventually, I told the class about Mary-Lou. I realised that if I was to teach about authentic leadership, I needed to be authentic. I referred to the work of Simon Sinek and that of Brene Brown. At times I think the students thought I was mad - but at the end, the module was very well evaluated.

I remember a particularly lively session not long after I had told the class about Mary-Lou. The energy in the room was high. We had been talking about resilience and about making improvements to healthcare. This required vitality. The students were up for it. But they were going to need support. Too many newly qualified nurses leave the profession within the first eighteen months. They are disillusioned and burned out. In that moment, in class, I realised that the strategies required for making the transition from student to professional had similarities with my experience of navigating grief. As a starting point, learning to prioritise self-care is a MUST. Before Lou died, I had never prioritised self-care. But since then, I've learned that looking after myself first gives me the energy to support others. I realised there were many things I had learned in navigating grief that could support newly qualified nurses. The purpose of Mary's Place® was becoming clear.

As if I needed further evidence, I suddenly remembered my PhD research. Some years earlier, I had been exploring transition and the concept of liminality: the unsettling, in-between phase of transformation. I had even co-authored a paper on it with Mary-Lou (Crane and Abbott, 2021). It was the missing piece of the jigsaw. I felt confident that I had finally found my niche. Mary's Place® would be a community of support and empowerment for newly qualified nurses. At first, I thought this was just a nursing issue. But in speaking to others, I realised teachers, solicitors, and other professionals were facing the same struggles. The problem wasn't necessarily the profession, it was the transition into the profession. I knew Mary-Lou would have agreed. She had shared an insightful message on Facebook, just weeks before she died, in response to the general election result. In this post, she paid tribute to hardworking NHS and teaching staff. Lou was also a Law graduate, so the potential to eventually reach out to solicitors felt right. I envisioned a space where new professionals (regardless of their field) realise that challenges exist in every profession, and no one has to navigate them alone. I imagined conversations between teachers, solicitors and nurses going something like:

"Well at least I am unlikely to kill someone" (teachers and solicitors)

"I am glad I do not need to go to court" (nurses and teachers)

"I could not manage a class of children" (solicitors and nurses).

Mary's Place® was formally established as a Community Interest Company in August 2023. Whilst I believe there is merit in sharing learning across professions, I realised this was an aspiration for the future. We needed to start small, and the natural place to start was with nurses. Our intention is to trial a teacher's programme later in 2025. Interestingly, the name Mary's Place® had never been in doubt. Mary-Lou and I are Bruce Springsteen fans. Bruce and the E Street Band had played 'Mary's Place' at Lou's first concert (aged 6 years old). I still remember her saying "Mummy, they are playing my song". It is a lovely memory.

What do we do at Mary's Place®?

Our mission is to support newly qualified professionals as they make the transition from student to professional. Mary's Place® offers face-to-face and online support. We provide one-to-one coaching sessions, peer support and well-being day retreats. Our retreat days typically comprise a yoga session and a sound bath. We combine these restorative, relaxing practices with coaching, peer support sessions and refreshment breaks. The days are exceptionally well evaluated:

"Mary's Place, I will call the 'ME' place. A very awesome opportunity to reflect and relax away from the busy schedules at work. The best place to spend your day off and rejuvenate."

"Another amazing day at Mary's Place! I went full to the brim with stress and anxieties regarding my career and overall life

and have left feeling so much lighter, with a clear head and excited for the future. The day provides so much relaxation and food for thought, such a good investment in your own well-being."

Essentially, Mary's Place® responds to the needs of our participants. To provide some structure, early in this journey, I developed a framework which I called GRACE. I am not entirely sure where this came from, grace is not a word I use frequently. I have chosen to believe it was another of those things that was meant to be...

For Mary's Place® GRACE stands for gratitude, reflection, awareness, community and empowerment. During my training as a mindfulness and resilience coach, I discovered Martin Seligman's work on **gratitude** as part of the positive psychology movement. In brief (we discuss this much more in workshops) it is important to notice things that go well and be grateful for these moments. In life (and especially in nursing) we are trained to be on high alert for things going wrong. Re-training the brain to notice positive aspects of life has been proven to improve feelings of well-being. Gratitude, therefore, is our starting point at Mary's Place®.

The Nursing and Midwifery Council (Nursing's professional body) requires us to practice **reflection.** At Mary's Place® we predominantly reflect on the positive aspects of nursing practice. Typically, we invite participants to reflect upon good things that have happened at work. Regardless of how seemingly insignificant. This activity fits very well with gratitude practice, and whilst it sounds basic, the power of the exercise is surprising. It is all too easy for nurses to remember only the things they have forgotten to do on a shift. Actively reflecting on the positive things that happen, reinforces achievements. These two elements contribute to developing a greater awareness of the importance of nursing practice. This encourages staff to remember the value of the work that they do.

Reflection is an excellent learning tool but can lead to staff being self-critical. One component of the **awareness** part of GRACE is to notice when we are being self-critical. When this happens, staff are invited to exercise self-compassion. In a self-compassion activity, staff might be asked to consider a situation in which they wish they had acted differently. We do not dwell on this, rather we use it as a prompt. Staff are then invited to write down how they might speak to a colleague who had taken the same action. We are almost always more kind to colleagues than we are to ourselves. This exercise reminds us of that.

Community is the essence of Mary's Place®. Being a newly qualified professional can be lonely. It is easy to think that everyone else knows what they are doing whilst you are floundering. Once you get into this type of negative spiral, it doesn't take long for you to think that you must be in the wrong job. A supportive community in which members share their challenges results in staff feeling less lonely. Whilst I love supporting newly qualified nurses, there is nothing better than seeing them support each other. Mary's Place® provides the 'brave' space for peers to share concerns and solutions.

Empowerment, this is our overall goal. The practical focus at

Mary's Place® is self-care and support. But the ultimate intention is that we encourage a generation of new nurses who are empowered. These individuals will understand the importance of filling their own cup first. They will then be better placed to support the person next to them. One of the current problems is that the workforce is exhausted. Cups are well and truly broken, not just empty. We are amid a worldwide nursing and healthcare crisis. Mary's Place® cannot change that. But what we CAN do is to empower our new professionals to look after themselves. Ultimately, this will lead to future managers understanding the importance of self-care. Supporting colleagues will be the norm. This is the basis of cultivating a successful team. I believe that small changes are possible, even in a crisis.

A recent comment from a Mary's Place® attendee provides a lovely summary:

"Mary's Place is inspirational. Mary's Place helped me to improve and focus on my own well-being as I started my nursing career, so I can be the best nurse possible for my patients!"

Future Plans

Mary's Place® continues to evolve. Our Facebook group is growing. In response to requests for face-to-face meetings, we plan to offer informal café drop-in sessions during 2025. The University of Central Lancashire has conducted a survey on our behalf to better understand the needs of new graduates with regards to transition. The national reach of the questionnaire has further raised awareness of the presence of Mary's Place® which is exciting and scary at the same time.

Without a doubt, our well-being retreats have been the most popular activity. Retreat days were funded through donations from our supporters and hosted by Healing Time in Birkenhead, Merseyside. A small number of nurses were sponsored to attend by their employer, but most joined on their day off. The days were exceptionally well-evaluated, but we recognised that it would be even better if Mary's Place® retreat days could be delivered in 'work time'...

To facilitate this ambitious goal, we jumped at the opportunity to partner with The University Hospital's Liverpool Group (UHLG) and apply for The Royal College of Nursing Foundation Amin Abdullah Award 2024.

We won!

This success validates and adds credibility to the work we are doing at Mary's Place®. It also raises awareness of the support needs of newly qualified professionals. The Amin Abdullah Award will fund Mary's Place® well-being days as part of UHLG's preceptorship programme during 2025.

Now that Mary's Place® is growing, I felt it was important that I had a formal coaching qualification to ensure our young professionals are in safe hands. I thus completed an ILM Level 7 Executive Coaching and Mentoring Course. Also, to ensure flexibility in being able to deliver 'in-house' well-being, I have added sound healing to my list of qualifications! It is a magical healing modality which I love to deliver. I love that my healing journey continues whilst I support others. All in Mary-Lou's name.

Some final thoughts

There is no doubt in my mind—if I had the choice, Mary-Lou would still be here, living her best life, making the changes she dreamed of. I would trade everything for that reality. But I can't change what happened. What I can do is choose how I respond. And I choose to honour Mary-Lou by making a difference in another way. Some days, grief still knocks me off my feet. I expect it always will. But I do have better days. I love seeing newly qualified nurses leave Mary's Place® events feeling re-energised and empowered. I smile when I hear a newly qualified nurse say, "I don't feel so alone now". On those days, I know we are doing something important. I see Mary-Lou in every nurse who rediscovers their confidence. In every professional who finds their feet. In every person who takes a deep breath and decides to keep going. Lou's impact continues—not just in memory, but in action. And if there's one thing I want others to take from this, it's that even in the darkest moments, we still have the power to create something meaningful.

We may not control what happens to us, but we always have the power to choose how we move forward. Mary-Lou's kindness and determination live on in Mary's Place®, a legacy of support, strength, and empowerment.

If you believe in supporting the next generation of professionals, you are already part of the Mary's Place® movement. Whether you're a nurse, a teacher, or simply someone who believes in lifting others up, we'd love for you to be involved. Let's make sure no one navigates their early career alone.

How to Get Involved

- Know any newly qualified nurses? Let them know we are here.
- We're building a teachers' waitlist—get in touch if you'd like to help shape this program.
- Want to support? Every voice, every action, every bit of support makes a difference.

The best way to get in touch is through the website

Website: www.marys-place.co.uk

Resources

Crane, J & Abbott, M-L 2021, 'Mind the gap: The relationship between liminality, learning and leaving in pre-registration nurse education', Nurse Education in Practice, vol. 50, 102952. https://doi.org/10.1016/j.nepr.2020.102952 Miller, K. 2019 '14 Benefits of Practicing Gratitude'. **Positive Psychology.com Available at:** https://positivepsychology.com/benefits-of-gratitude/

If you wish to donate to Mary's Place®

www.justgiving.com/crowdfunding/MarysPlace2024

Biography

Julie Bilboe-Crane is an experienced Nurse Lecturer and Executive Coach. She is also CEO of Mary's Place®, a non-profit company she established to support newly qualified professionals as they make the transition from student to professional.

GRIT AND GRACE

"HEALING DOESN'T MEAN THE PAIN
DISAPPEARS—IT MEANS YOU LEARN TO
HOLD IT WITH LOVE AND WALK
FORWARD WITH STRENGTH."

Unknown

GRIT AND GRACE

CHAPTER 6
BY LARA PENNINGTON

The Secret to Chasing Big Dreams? Grit, Growth & the Courage to Embrace Change

I admit I've lived a pretty wild, exciting & adventurous life but it hasn't all been sunshine & rainbows, there's also been plenty of bad weather, storms & even a couple of earthquakes (metaphorically & literally).

* I've lived in the UK, Czech Republic, Spain, Thailand & the Philippines, I've spent a lot of time in Cuba & South East Asia, backpacked through every continent (except Antarctica) & flown business class around-the-world many, many times.

* Career-wise I've reinvented myself over & over: I've worked in shops, bars, hotels, a ski-resort, as a Lifeguard, Waterskiing Instructor & English Teacher, I spent several decades in corporate as an International Marketing Director, was a partner in an Asian tech start-up & founded a Life & Career Coaching company for midlife women.

Two mottos have guided me throughout my life, shaping my choices, fuelling my resilience, & helping me embrace the unpredictable beauty of reinvention:

1. **Life is too short to...** feel stuck, bored, or unhappy. We only get one shot at this adventure called life, so why spend it settling for anything less than fabulous? For me, this motto has always been a wake-up call, a nudge to step out of my comfort zone & chase what truly energises me.

2. **If you can Dream it, you can Do it!** This isn't just a catchy phrase; it's a belief that has carried me through countless challenges. Dreaming big is about imagining a life without limits & daring to take the steps to make it real, no matter how impossible it may seem at the start.

These mottos didn't just spring to life overnight, they were forged through experiences, challenges, & lessons learned. As I've journeyed through the highs & lows, three key traits have become my superpowers, helping me thrive no matter what life throws my way:

1. **Grit:** To me, grit is more than determination; it's a blend of passion & perseverance that keeps you moving forward, even when the path is rocky. Life

has thrown its fair share of curveballs my way, pushing my resilience to its limits. Yet, I've learned to pick myself up after every setback, stronger & more focused. Grit is my number one superpower, the force that keeps me grounded & moving forward.

2. **Embracing Change:** Change is inevitable, but learning to embrace it has been a game-changer for me. At first, I resisted it, because who wouldn't want to keep things stable & under control? But over time, I realized that letting go of control is liberating. Change brings growth, & growth brings success & happiness. Now, I welcome change with open arms, knowing it often signals the start of something exciting.

3. **Dreaming Big:** I've always loved an adventure, & dreaming big is my way of keeping that spirit alive. To me, it's about setting goals that stretch the imagination, goals that seem out of reach at first. It's about pushing beyond limitations & daring to ask, "What if?" Dreaming big isn't just about ambition; it's about living a life full of love, laughter, adventure & impact. Work hard, play hard, dream big & give back - that's my mantra.

Grit Fuels Change & Change Fuels Dreams! These mottos & traits have inspired me to live boldly, bravely, authentically, & confidently. When we hit midlife, things change - we change, our lives change, & what we want changes! What was important in our 20s is usually very different from what we want in our 40s & 50s. But the biggest thing holding midlife women back from happiness, following our dreams, & achieving our goals is often ourselves!

I've been there & understand the challenges women face in combining a career we love with the life we want! That's why I help midlife women who are feeling stuck, stressed & scared, to revamp their lives & careers & discover "what's next?"

Is there MORE to life?

I grew up in the UK, in a relatively typical middle class British village & like most families, it had its ups & downs:

* The ups - a close-knit family, living in a big, country house with horses, by the golf course & going to an exclusive school with similarly privileged friends. I was lucky to experience "how the other half lives" as it gave me an insight into how money can be amazing to achieve certain goals, but it most definitely doesn't guarantee happiness.

* The downs - parents messy divorce, downsizing, moving away & going to a huge state school where I was the odd one out, didn't fit in & was bullied for being too posh. The change was dramatic & I hated it, but my resilience & adaptability kicked in for the first time, & by my second year, I'd been voted Head Girl & House Captain of the sports teams. Generous allowances were a luxury from my previous life so I had to work at a Fish & Chip shop on the weekends, which has to be one of the worst part-time jobs - smelling of fried fish & a nightmare for teenage skin! But I soon learned another important lesson - "What doesn't break you, makes you stronger!"

As a teenager, I was already craving something more - a sense of adventure & freedom.

After A levels, I'd dreamed of taking a "gap year" & travelling the world, much to my mother's amusement & she was quick to squash the idea - "You haven't worked hard enough yet to need a gap year". So, I pivoted to a more "parent-friendly" option & moved to Madrid to learn Spanish instead.

Madrid in the 1980s was everything I didn't know I needed. It was fabulously exotic - vibrant streets, rich culture, & a pace of life that felt worlds away from the UK. Back then, hardly anyone spoke English, so I had no choice but to dive headfirst into the language & the culture. I loved every moment of it. My first year in Madrid confirmed something within me: I wasn't EVER going back to the UK.

Of course, Mum had other plans. "If you don't go to university, you'll struggle to achieve your goals," reminding me of my dream to work in media & marketing. Begrudgingly, I returned to the UK & enrolled at Manchester University, but although I spent the academic year studying in England, the other four months of the year I escaped back to Spain & worked as a water-skiing instructor on the Costa Brava, jetting around in a speed boat, basking in the sun & loving life.

Even during university, my adventurous streak was strong. When it came time for my work placement, I chose Prague - back when it was still Czechoslovakia. It was like stepping back in time, an experience that was as challenging as it was eye-opening. I'd been a vegetarian for years but that wasn't an option in the family I lived with - it was pork every single day, my usual supply of exotic fresh fruit & veg just wasn't available, so Mum sent packages of vitamin C & I had to adapt or starve! The contrast between the familiarity of home & the starkly different world of Prague only fuelled my desire to embrace the unfamiliar.

After graduating, I knew there was no question about where I wanted to be. I packed my bags & moved to Barcelona, a city that would become my home for the next two decades, & where I still call home, even though I've since lived all over the world. Barcelona was everything I'd dreamed of & more. It was where I built my career in international media & marketing (thanks Mum, you were right) & I thrived in the fast-paced, dynamic environment. I travelled the world for work, collaborated with incredible people, & built a life that, for many years, seemed perfect.

But perfection is often an illusion. As I entered my 40s as a single mum with a young child & a fast-paced corporate career, I was struggling to balance it all. Long days in the office (in an old fashioned toxic, male-dominated, environment) & international travel every month just weren't compatible with solo parenting, self-care, or any semblance of a social life. Niggling doubts began to creep in & I found myself lying awake at night, wondering if this was it. I'd achieved so much, but something was missing. The spark that had always driven me, the one that had pushed me to leave the UK, move to Spain & chase adventure, was fading. I began asking myself some big questions: Is this all there is? Can I do this for another 20 years? Could there be more to life than the career I'd built?

That restlessness marked the beginning of a new chapter,

although I didn't know it yet. Looking back, I wonder how things would have turned differently if I hadn't been brave enough to say, "Hell yeah, what's next?" & follow my dreams.

Eat, Pray, Love

Sometimes, life gives us a little nudge that we need to make some changes, but we often push it away, procrastinate & worry but don't take action. Other times, change happens because it smacks us over the head with a sledgehammer & there's no turning back. My midlife turning point was the latter.

It began with an emergency room visit, a wake-up call I couldn't ignore. Burnout had pushed me to my limit, & it was clear that something had to give. The stress of managing a high-flying corporate career, juggling the demands of single motherhood, & trying to maintain a semblance of balance had caught up with me. My body was screaming for a change, & for the first time, I truly listened.

Making the decision to leave my job wasn't easy. Fear loomed large. What would people think if I walked away from a "perfect" career? What would I do? Could I even afford to? These questions kept me up at night, but deep down, I knew staying stuck wasn't an option.

I'll never forget the moment I decided to take the leap. I asked myself what I'd do if I had a magic wand - I realized I wanted more: more happiness, more connection, more freedom & I also wanted that gap year I'd missed out on! So, with two backpacks & round-the-word tickets, my 7-year-old son & I embarked on what I fondly call my "Eat, Pray, Love" adventure. It was terrifying & exhilarating all at once but ultimately life-changing & my best, crazy decision ever!

We spent a year travelling from Europe, through the Americas & across South East Asia, just the two of us & our Lonely Planet travel guides! I quickly realized travel planning, full-time parenting & home-schooling were often tougher than my insanely stressful old job! Contrary to popular belief, it wasn't about running away, it was about rediscovering myself. I had the space to breathe, dream, let go of the corporate identity I'd clung to for so long & reflect on who I was now & what I truly wanted.

That was the first of my midlife career revamps, but not the last ...

My next adventure took us to the Philippines, where I threw myself, head first into the tech start-up world, an unexpected but exciting chapter. The entrepreneurial spirit was contagious, & for the first time in years, I felt alive. My doubts about leaving my corporate career began to fade as I realized I could build something meaningful on my terms & surrounded with like-minded people.

Our adventure expanded again in Thailand, where I faced yet another leap of faith - becoming a partner in an Asian tech start-up. It was daunting, but by then, I'd learned to trust my instincts & say "hell yeah, bring it on!" Asia was where I truly started to rebuild, piece by piece, a life & career that aligned with who I was becoming & what was important to me.

These experiences weren't without challenges. Homeschooling a seven-year-old while travelling, building a business & making friends in foreign countries while navigating new languages & cultures was no small feat, & there were plenty of moments where I doubted myself. But every obstacle reinforced my resilience. I discovered that when you're willing to take bold steps, the universe often meets you halfway.

Looking back, my "Eat, Pray, Love" chapter wasn't an escape, it was a reinvention. It was about shedding the expectations I'd carried for so long & stepping into a life that felt authentic & aligned. It set the stage for what came next & proved to me that change, no matter how daunting, is always worth it when it leads you closer to who you truly are.

If we can DREAM it, we can DO it!

Nearly a decade later, I found myself at another crossroads. Asia had become the backdrop for my reinvention. Surrounded by entrepreneurial energy, I discovered the thrill of building something from scratch, it wasn't just about climbing a corporate ladder anymore, it was about creating something meaningful, something that aligned with my values.

But even in this exciting environment, I knew deep down that I wasn't finished evolving & after years of building someone else's dream, I wanted to create my own.

Then came the global upheaval of COVID, which became a turning point for me once again, Asia was hit hard & early so we decamped back to Europe for a while.

Locked down in Spain, with time to reflect, I noticed a pattern: the women I met, worked with, & mentored often felt stuck.

They were juggling careers, families, & dreams they'd long since shelved. Their struggles mirrored my own, & I started to wonder: what if I could help others navigate these same challenges I had? I was turning 50 & realized it was now or never, so I made the leap & retrained as an Executive & Career Coach with the International Coaching Federation, it was one of the best decisions I've ever made & I wish I'd done it sooner!

Launching *Evolve & Thrive* was both thrilling & terrifying. There were moments when my impostor syndrome was strong & loud, questioning whether I could really succeed in this new venture. But every doubt was countered by the belief that I was exactly where I needed to be. Each client I worked with, each small victory, solidified my confidence.

I've poured everything I have into this life & career revamp - drawing from my 25+ years in business, my personal experiences of reinvention, & my passion for helping women thrive.

Coaching isn't just a career shift; it feels like a calling, I'm creating an inclusive community where women can dream big & confidently build the lives they truly want.

This new phase of my life hasn't been without challenges. Building a business from scratch comes with its fair share of financial hurdles, late nights, & moments of self-doubt. But every time I hear a client say, "wow, I feel so much better, and much more confident," it reminds me why I started this journey, & that when we follow our instincts & trust ourselves, amazing things can happen, because if we can DREAM it, we can DO it!

Evolve & Thrive

Founding *Evolve & Thrive* isn't just about reinventing my own life, because for me, it's not just a business - it's a movement. It's about empowering women to rediscover their strengths & align with their values, to rewrite their stories, step into bold new versions of themselves & embrace the exciting possibilities of midlife.

What I've also learned along the way is that the impact goes far beyond the individual. Each woman who chooses to rewrite her story creates a ripple effect. She inspires her family, her friends & her colleagues. I've seen clients leave toxic workplaces to launch businesses that align with their passions & I've watched others negotiate promotions or career changes that previously seemed impossible. In every story, there's a shared theme: the courage to take the first step & believe in what's possible.

As I look ahead & dream big, I see *Evolve & Thrive* becoming more than just a coaching practice. I envision a global hub for midlife reinvention, a community where women from around the world can come together to share their stories, support each other, & access resources that empower them to thrive. From workshops to retreats, the possibilities are endless. And the best part is, we've only just gotten started!

On a personal level, my vision isn't just about professional growth, it's about balance & joy. I've learned that thriving means creating space for the things that make life meaningful: family, adventure, & connection. Whether it's paddleboarding with my son, reading in the hot-tub or a glass of wine with friends, these moments fuel the work I do &

remind me of my why & what's really important to me.

The future is bright, & I'm endlessly excited for what's to come. If there's one thing I've learned, it's that reinvention isn't just a possibility, it's a choice & when we choose to dream big & take bold steps, we open ourselves to a world of opportunity.

Life's too short...

Midlife isn't a crisis; it's a calling. A time to redefine what success, happiness, & fulfilment look like for you. If my story resonates, let it be a spark for your own transformation.

So, here's my challenge for you: Take the first step. Maybe it's as simple as asking yourself, "What do I really, really want?" or maybe it's reaching out to someone who can help you uncover your next chapter.

Whatever it is, don't wait, because life's too short to be unhappy at work or stuck in a career you've fallen out of love with … & change starts with a single decision.

I'd love to invite you to join our Evolve & Thrive Tribe, a community of bold, inspiring women ready to cheer you on as you rewrite your story.

Or take the leap & schedule a "Get UNSTUCK" call with me. Let's uncover your dreams, your goals, & the path to your next big adventure.

Because if you can DREAM it, you can DO it! & there's no better time to start than NOW 🌐

If I sound like the kind of coach you'd like in your corner

then I'd love to talk with you. Why not schedule a free, no-obligation call with me and we can chat about your career challenges and how I can help you.

Let's Chat!

EVOLVE & THRIVE TRIBE

I'd also love to invite you to join the Evolve & Thrive Tribe on Facebook:

www.facebook.com/groups/evolvethrivetribe

We're a dynamic group of amazing midlife women who want MORE from life: freedom, success, balance, happiness, and fun! Together, we're a powerhouse of support and empowerment, cheering each other on to thrive both in our professional and personal lives. It's a space to grow, laugh, share, and shine, surrounded by like-minded women who totally get it! I look forward to meeting you there!

"LIFE'S TOO SHORT TO BE UNHAPPY AT
WORK OR STUCK IN A CAREER YOU'VE
FALLEN OUT OF LOVE WITH!"

Lara Pennington

GRIT AND GRACE

CHAPTER 7

BY LISA ADAMS

Wounds to Wisdom

The sterile smell of antiseptic, the quiet beeping of monitors, and the hushed whispers of concerned families had become my everyday reality. As a Registered Nurse, I had dedicated my life to healing others, but somewhere along the way, I had lost myself. The weight of suffering clung to me, unseen yet suffocating. I had spent years witnessing trauma-watching life slip away in acute hospital wards, holding hands with patients as they took their last breaths, zipping up countless body bags, and carrying the grief of families who had just lost a loved one. The emotional toll of nursing had become unbearable. I wasn't just exhausted; I was spiritually depleted.

I had spent my entire career in a world that demanded constant action, organising, decision-making, and resilience-all qualities typically associated with masculine energy. I was always giving, always caring, always on call, pushing through exhaustion, running on adrenaline, and silencing my own needs in the name of service. Being physically abused-punched, kicked or spat on trying to assess my patients, had become a regular occurrence. And yet, no matter how much I gave, it was never enough. I had become disconnected from myself, from my body, and from my intuition.

Day One

Nursing is often described as a calling, an active service that requires compassion, resilience, and an unwavering commitment to patient care. But beneath the sterile hallways and the beeping machines on the endless shift rotations, there exists an unspoken burden: the suppression of emotions. We were expected to remain composed in the face of suffering, to be a steady presence when patients and families fall apart. Yet, what happens when the very emotions we push aside begin to fester?

From day one, as a young nineteen-year-old student nurse, I was conditioned to prioritise others over myself. Training emphasised clinical competence, professionalism, and emotional restraint. Showing too much emotion can be perceived as weakness, a loss of control, and highly unprofessional. In high stakes environments like busy wards, there is little time to process grief or fear. A patient passes, a family sobs, and within moments, a nurse must move on to her next task.

Over time, this suppression becomes second nature. Nurses learn to compartmentalise, to pack away their pain in the invisible storage of their minds, believing they will unpack it later, but later rarely comes. Instead, the weight of unprocessed sorrow and stress accumulates, settling in the body like an unseen illness. Pain has a way of shaping us. Trauma, whether sudden or prolonged, leaves its mark-not just on our minds but on our bodies, our choices, and the way we see the world. Trauma is more than just a painful memory; it is an imprint on the nervous system. It lingers in the body, manifesting as tension, fatigue, or illness. But trauma does not have to be the end of the story. It can be the beginning of something else-something deeper, wiser, and even more beautiful. Transformation is not about erasing the past but about alchemizing it, turning suffering into strength and wounds into wisdom.

When The Heart Can't Take Anymore

The decision to walk away from a thirty-year career in nursing was not an easy one. It was my identity, my source of stability, my purpose-or so I thought. But my soul was screaming for something different, something more. It was calling me home-to myself, to my feminine essence, to a life of softness, intuition, and flow. The breaking point didn't come suddenly. It was slow and insidious. It built up over time, one loss after another, one sleepless night blending into the next, one too many days spent caring for others while neglecting myself.

I remember one shift where a young woman was gravely ill and her mother had been called in as an emergency, time was running out for her beloved daughter. Anxiously, I hovered around the entrance to the ward, knowing her mother was going to be met by the devasting news her girl wasn't going to make it. Words that no parent wants to hear ever. Holding her mum's hand, we watched her daughter's life slowly slip away, and there was nothing I could do to change that. Witnessing the trauma of a mother losing her child brought thoughts of my own little girl, tears began to stream down my cheeks and the emotional restraint I had been trained to do, could no longer be contained. What I haven't told you is that her mother was in a wheelchair. On noticing my distress, she stood out of her wheelchair and shuffled across the short distance between us, wrapping her arms around me, consoling me, relative to nurse, mother to mother, woman to woman and human to human. The opposite of everything I had been trained to do.

Something inside me broke that night.

I drove home in silence, numb. My hands trembled on the steering wheel, my body exhausted, but my mind racing. I had spent years witnessing all this pain, absorbing their grief, and carrying the weight of lives lost. But who was holding space for me? Who was healing me?

The answer was clear: no one. Everything inside me whispered: it's time to leave.

Choosing To Heal

I had never learned how to hold space for myself. I had never learned how to receive, how to surrender, how to allow softness into my life. I had spent so long in survival mode and the 'doing' masculine energy, that I had forgotten how to simply be. That night, I made the decision that changed everything: I was going to reclaim myself. Healing begins when we recognise that our emotions are not a burden, but a sign of our humanity. To care for others, we must also care for ourselves. Only then can we continue to serve not as empty vessels, but as compassionate, whole beings.

Transformation begins with a choice: the decision to face what has been buried, to step into the discomfort of healing rather than the familiarity of suffering. This is not an easy choice. It requires courage because healing asks to feel what we once suppressed, to sit with pain instead of running from it. Healing is not linear. Some days will feel like progress, others like regression. But every moment of awareness, every small act of self-compassion, is a step towards wholeness.

Leaving nursing felt like free falling. For so long I had been defined by my role as a caregiver, and without it, I felt lost.

But in the emptiness, something else emerged, something ancient, powerful, and deeply feminine. I started listening to my own body. I began to honour my natural rhythms instead of forcing myself into burnout. I embraced my emotions instead of suppressing them. I reconnected with my sensuality, my creativity, and my intuition. I allowed myself to rest, to receive, to be supported. Understanding that breaking free from the cycle of emotional repression starts with acknowledgement.

For the first time in my life, I felt alive in acknowledging and honouring myself.

The Wisdom of The Womb

Leaving nursing was the greatest act of self-love I have ever done. It was a return to myself, to my essence, to my truth. I no longer live in survival mode. I live in trust. I no longer push and force. I flow. I no longer silence my desires. I honour them. And the journey I took to get here may surprise you. It was the journey through my womb. Yes, you read that right sister, my womb.

Our womb is where we hold and store our life experiences, emotions and trauma. The journey through the womb to wholeness is a sacred return to the essence of the woman we are, to our divine feminine. It is a passage through the deepest waters of creation, where we are formed not just in body but in spirit. Within the womb, we are cradled in divine love, untouched by the world's weight, connected to the pulse of the universe itself. Birth is not just an entrance into the physical realm-it is the beginning of a lifelong unfolding, a remembering of the wholeness we once knew. As we navigate the trials and transformations of life, we are called to reclaim that original harmony, shedding illusions of separation and awakening to the truth that we have never been broken. The journey through the womb to wholeness is to embrace the cycles of birth death and rebirth within us, surrendering to the divine flow that has carried us from the very beginning.

And here's the magic! We can rebirth ourselves over and over again, time after time, after time. You see, our womb is not just for creating babies and birthing their life. It is a power portal to creating our own lives, to birth the life we wish to bring into existence for ourselves. I invite you to pause for a moment here, to think about the life you are creating for yourself, are you still carrying dreams and desires waiting to be birthed?

The path of the feminine is a homecoming, a return to the way of the woman. And once you embrace it, life will never be the same. Living in the feminine way means trusting the unseen, the inner knowing that speaks in whispers rather than shouts. Intuition is a voice of the feminine, a deep-seated wisdom that arises when we quiet the mind and listened to the body. In a world driven by logic and external validation, intuition is often dismissed. Intuition is what our ancestors were burnt at the stake for expressing. We are taught to seek answers outside of ourselves, to follow rules, data and structure. But the feminine way asked us to tune inward-to trust that the body holds truth, that emotions are messengers, and that not everything can or should be rationalised.

Taking Life by The Ovaries

When I transformed my inner world, my outer world began to shift as well. I realised that I could create a life and business from a place of ease, flow, and feminine power. Instead of hustling, I allowed. Instead of chasing, I aligned. Instead of forcing, I surrendered. I created a life and business that felt nourishing, not depleting. A business rooted in my soul's desires, not society's expectations. A business that honoured my feminine essence, my cycles and my intuition. And now, I help other women to do the same.

Living in the way of the woman means trusting the unseen, the inner knowing that speaks in whispers rather than shouts.

Intuition is a voice of the womb, a deep-seated wisdom that arises when we quiet the mind and listened to the body and soul. In a world driven by logic and external validation, intuition is often dismissed. We are taught to seek answers outside of ourselves, to follow rules, data, and structure. But the feminine way asked us to tune inward- to trust that the body holds truth, that emotions are messengers, and that not everything can or should be rationalised.

Through my services I guide women back home to themselves, because your body is your home and you must always return to her. I empower women to remember their magic, to show them that success doesn't have to come from burnout. To teach them that their feminine energy is their greatest power, that is strength in softness, though the world often tells us otherwise. We are conditioned to believe that power lies in aggression, dominance, emotional suppression and unshakable resolve. But the feminine way reveals another kind of power-the power of presence, of deep listening, of nurturing and compassion. The feminine way teaches that vulnerability is not something to be feared but embraced. It is through our openness and connection that transformation occurs.

Perhaps the most challenging and liberating aspects of living in the feminine way is surrender. In a world that equates control with success, surrender feels like a risk but the feminine knows that true freedom comes not from grasping but from releasing- from trusting the natural unfolding of life. Surrender is not giving up; It is giving over. It is the deep exhale that comes when we realise, we do not have to do it all, that we are supported, that we are part of something greater. It is allowing the universe to meet us halfway, to trust that what is meant for us will come, and that what leaves was never ours to hold.

Made of Magic

YOU lady are made of magic! It's time to connect to the ancient feminine wisdom of your womb and a remembering of your power. Your empowerment is your inner strength that enables you to live your life fully. It is your natural ability to take charge of your life and make it happen. The womb itself is cyclical, working in harmony with the cycles of the moon, a 28-day menstrual cycle is connected to the 28-day Lunar cycle. Each phase has its own energy and own gifts. Each phase has its own signs and symptoms that might arise when we are not looking after our body, living cyclically and honouring all aspects of ourselves.

The good news is that the womb is a resilient and robust organ that various practices and techniques can heal. Womb healing is not only a process but also a journey, and a path back to yourself. The womb can regenerate itself every month, and so can you.

Here is where the real magic lies. Even if your womb has been removed, her energetical blueprint within your womb space still holds all her power. This is your power portal, your medicine bowl, and your cauldron. There is a wisdom so powerful in your womb, that not even trauma can restrain it. Trauma can have a profound impact on the physical and emotional health of your womb. The womb is not just a physical organ but a centre of emotional and spiritual energy. An essential part of your healing journey involves taking intentional steps to nurture your physical, emotional and spiritual wellbeing. By prioritising self-care, you can create a supportive internal environment that promotes healing and restoration.

I spent decades pushing through exhaustion, running on adrenaline, and silencing my own needs in the name of service. To care for others in my role as a nurse, while abandoning my own needs. But here's the thing. The pelvic bowl is home to the only 'optional' organ system in a woman's body. The Reproductive System. If the body needs to combat physiological stress by conserving energy- what's the first system to be shut down? The one that could endanger its very existence by making another life, a baby. Tension here means that the body can't move things, like energy and toxins out, and can't let things in. We are left with symptoms and conditions such as fertility challenges, Endometriosis, Polycystic Ovaries, Fibroids, Irritable Bowel Syndrome, painful periods, irregular cycle, Pelvic Inflammatory Disease, hormonal imbalances, chronic bladder infections and Anorgasmia. Does any of this sound familiar to you?

Life is busy and women have a never ending 'to-do' list, being conditioned to be everything to everyone. Here's the catch, when a woman lives primarily in masculine energy, rooted in constant doing, achieving, and pushing forward-her body begins to suffer. The feminine essence thrives in flow, intuition, rest, and receptivity, but when forced into a cycle of hustle and rigidity, the nervous system becomes overworked, stress hormones surge, and the natural rhythms of the body are disrupted. This disconnection can manifest as burnout, hormonal imbalances, chronic fatigue, a loss of emotional and spiritual alignment. The feminine body is designed to ebb and flow, to honour cycles of creation and rest, yet modern society often demands a pace that denies this truth. Healing comes when a woman softens into her natural essence, allowing space for nourishment, creativity, and surrender. By reclaiming your feminine energy, you restore balance, vitality, and the deep sacred connection to your own body and soul. I invite you to enquire within, are you honouring your body and soul with this right now?

For Goddess Sake

For Goddess sake, it's time to stop playing small. Are you ready to unleash and ignite deeper possibilities and potential, from the inside out, for lasting results? Do you feel called to sync with the natural rhythms of your body, exploring your womb health, healing, and creating an aligned life? Are you ready to take the first steps towards birthing your dream life, business, or finding your unique path? If so, please find Lisa's offerings below to work with her and create your own success story. From Yoga Beyond Poses, Sister Circles, Womb Healing, Shamanic Womb Massage, Luna & Love Retreats, to The Way of The Woman Mentoring, a bespoke offering is here to be created for your unique needs.

You don't have to do it alone. Lisa is here to guide and support you every step of the way, just like she has done with a tribe of other women who have joined her offerings. Lisa understands that women want to use their gifts to serve at a deeper level, knowing when they rise, they lift everyone else around them. Don't wait to create the life and business you've been dreaming of, reach out and let's get started on your journey back home to yourself.

The transformational journey from wounds to wisdom is not easy, but it is possible. And on the other side, there is not just healing. There is a returning to the wisdom that has always lived within you. There is wholeness. There is light. There is you, fully alive.

Connect with Lisa here:

Linktree: https://linktree/Lisaadamshomebodyhealing

Website: www.lisaadamshomebodyhealing.com

Facebook: Lisa Adams

Instagram: Lisaadamshomebodyhealing

LinkedIn: Lisa Adams

Email: support@lisaadamsmentoring.com

"WOMB HEALING IS MORE THAN JUST RECOVERY, IT'S A HOMECOMING TO THE DEEPEST PARTS OF YOURSELF."

Lisa Adams

GRIT AND GRACE

CHAPTER 8

BY LISA NUTLAND

How pregnant is VERY PREGNANT?

Hello, is that Miss Dunning? This is the nurse from the doctor's surgery, calling with your blood results. Your pregnancy test has come back positive! LIKE WHAT???? There must be some sort of mistake here, I'm on the pill and having regular periods. "I'm sorry but your blood results show high levels of the pregnancy hormone HCG, and you are VERY PREGNANT." Ironically I had been going back and forth, having difficulties losing weight. The blood test I thought I was having, was to check my thyroid function. Funny how I was struggling to lose weight!

So, this was how it all began! I can remember thinking 'This

CAN NOT be right!' I worked in a private nursery and absolutely adore children, but had certainly not made any plans to have any at that time. I was twenty-nine, in a stable relationship, but now just wasn't the right time. I popped into our local Asda to pick up a pregnancy test on the way home, still thinking that it just couldn't be possible. Hell, the blue line appeared in seconds, right in front of my eyes. I honestly felt sick! I'M PREGNANT, what do I do now?

I hardly slept that evening, the father seemed quite pleased, and we decided to get a doctor's appointment just to confirm, as I was still not sure this was real. I knew how pregnancy should feel, and I had no inkling or symptoms so it can't be real, can it? Two days later I walked into my doctor's surgery - back in the day when appointments were less like gold dust. "Yes, you are pregnant and VERY PREGNANT!" There it was again, how pregnant is VERY PREGNANT? "You need an emergency scan to determine the expected date."

This is going way to fast, in a week that started out pretty normal. My scan was booked for a week later, and that was a whole new level of experience.

The day of my scan arrived; I was nervous but curious

all rolled into one. Instructions beforehand stated that I had to drink a pint of fluid before my scan, and that's where the fun began. I was ready to burst by the time I was called into my appointment, to be told "Your bladder is too full, can you go and empty just a little bit." Have you ever tried sitting on the toilet, ready to burst and only being able to let out a LITTLE BIT? It's near on impossible, but I tried.

That moment the 'scan person' is looking at the screen with a scrunched-up face and your heart is in your mouth... "Would you like to see?" There's me expecting to see a tiny blob on the screen, as soon as the monitor was turned, Oh no! I nearly fell off the bed when I saw a fully formed tiny human kicking its legs and sucking its thumb! Yep, I'm pregnant and VERY PREGNANT! "Ummmmmmm how old is that?" I was 20 weeks and 5 days. What the hell, I was VERY PREGNANT just as everyone kept telling me. It was TRUE, it was REALITY and my god I was speechless. They printed off the scan picture for me, and I kept looking at it, cried a little and just couldn't take my eyes off the little human being inside me.

My pregnancy didn't quite go to plan and what followed certainly kept us all on our toes.

This pregnancy is a doddle, NOT!

The next few weeks proved to be very difficult with the start of a water infection leading into another water infection. My first hospital stay came at around twenty-four weeks, where I was admitted with a kidney infection that knocked me sideways. The pain and sickness was unbearable and I couldn't keep anything down.

My parental instinct kicked in, and I was petrified how being so poorly would affect my baby. My parents were by my side every day, and the dad popped in when he felt like it, usually making his work a priority. I spent that week trying to rest as much as possible, hooked up to drips and finally the infection subsided and I was allowed home, feeling better with a healthy baby.

Unfortunately, it didn't last around four weeks later at twenty-eight weeks, I was back in the hospital getting free bed & breakfast, with another water infection that hit me harder than the last one. This time I was very poorly and ended up having a private room from needing to be kept closely monitored, due to excessive pain and vomiting. It was a horrible, horrible time, but again we got through it. I had several scans that week and got to see the baby again which definitely made me feel more positive that we would both be okay. Another five day stay, and we were finally allowed home, and I left the hospital, straight to a scheduled midwife appointment. "Sorry Lisa, you have to straight back to the hospital." was NOT the words I wanted to hear. My urine dip test showed protein in my water, and my blood pressure was through the roof, which was the start of my next NIGHTMARE!

I felt like I had my own bed at the hospital with nurses greeting me with "Back again Lisa?" Not realising this would be my last time home for quite a while. I was diagnosed with pre-eclampsia which is a complication of pregnancy, causing high blood pressure, and high levels of protein in the urine that indicates kidney damage. Left untreated, pre-eclampsia can lead to serious, even fatal complications for both the mother and baby! I was beside myself with worry, but the hospital staff were amazing and reassured me that they would do their best for us both. My arms were suddenly full of cannulas with four drips attached. This was SERIOUS and I probably didn't realise just how much.

That evening around 11:30, I took a turn for the worse and was rushed to the delivery suite as my temperature spiked to over forty degrees and I began hallucinating. I shouldn't even consider laughing at this point, but I remember seeing the queen in my room, with Humpty Dumpty sitting on my window sill telling him "NO, DON'T JUMP"... There were doctors EVERYWHERE listening to me singing 'Humpty Dumpty sat on the wall, Humpty Dumpty had a great fall'... More fluids - which I have no idea what they were, were pumped into me and I heard "We might need to get this baby out TONIGHT."

At twenty-eight weeks, surely this was way too early, but I had to put all my trust and faith in the doctors who were trying to keep us both alive. We BOTH made it through the night, and I woke up in the delivery suite with a doctor telling me that they had managed to keep my blood pressure and temperature maintained within normal range, but I would have to stay in hospital for the rest of my pregnancy!

Twelve WEEKS? TWELVE WEEKS IN HOSPITAL OMG, NOOOOOOOOOOOOOOOOOOOOOO! But, if I had to be monitored to keep us both alive, what other option did I have? There was no option, so I started to get my head around the idea and come to terms with this being my new way of life for a while.

Having spent that evening, feeling quite emotional, the next few days tested me yet again. I slept okay that night but woke up feeling slightly 'off' but couldn't put my finger on it. I managed to get myself up and out of bed, to walk to the toilet and felt like a river had just erupted down my leg. OMG, I've just wet myself! I got myself straight back on the bed and called a nurse. "No, my lovely you haven't wet yourself, your waters have just broken." How could this be happening? I only found out I was pregnant 8 weeks ago and have been living an absolute nightmare since. Was this the start of my VERY early labour? What happens now? There were always so many questions as I tried to navigate all these ups and downs.

"Lisa, you will be fine! Bed rest can help regenerate your waters, we will monitor your waters with daily measuring scans and closely monitor the baby's movements! All will be fine! Unless you catch the infection strep B, then we will have to intervene and deliver the baby!" I could live with that, and the plan was to rest as much as possible to keep this baby cooking inside me for as long as possible.

I had best let everyone know what's happening, so my first phone call was to the baby's father, and it went just like this... "hi babes, just wanted to let you know that we are both okay but my waters have just broken! I have to bed rest and have daily scans to measure the fluid around the baby and the movements"...The response: "Okay, thanks for letting me know, I can't come to the hospital because Wales are playing football in Cardiff tonight, so I will see you in a couple of days!" I came off the phone, returned to my bed and sobbed my heart out. I should have realised then, that we weren't a priority and was definitely the start of the disaster about to unfold. My second phone call to my parents...

"We're on our way!" Was just what I needed to hear. They were my support, my love, my everything through this terrible time!

He shot out like a little Tornado

The following days I had several scans to monitor my water

and things were looking positive, baby was growing well and water remained at a safe level.

19th October 2002

Just under thirty weeks. The one infection I didn't want to catch, yes you guessed it... Here comes STREP B! Diagnosed through a blood test, and here we go yet again. The seriousness of this infection was the scariest.

Yet more drips attached, and the complications this incurs frightened me to death. 'WE have to get this baby out!'. I was being prepared for Labour. Injections to help develop the baby's lungs, antibiotics to stop the strep B from spreading to the baby and helping me fight the infection. I was tired, emotional, and scared but knew the fight in me had to do this! I had two days of fluids, antibiotics and injections, ready to be induced.

20th October 2002

9:30 am - We started with the pessary to soften my cervix.

4:30 pm - Then came the 'crochet hook' to break the waters. Neither really worked, so the plan was to move me to the delivery suite and start me on the SYNTO drip - A hormone drip used to induce a quick labour once the water is broken.

7:00 pm - my visit from the doctor and SCBU - special care baby unit staff. I was invited to go down to the SCBU unit to have a tour, as we were obviously going to need their expert support after the baby was born. This visit was the moment this all sank in for me, it frightened the absolute life out of me. I cried the whole time, and the realisation of what was about to happen hit me HARD. The staff were incredible and spoke to me with such gentle care and genuine concern. I returned to the ward and cried myself to sleep.

21st October 2002

11:30 am - I was moved into the delivery suite and introduced to my midwife who would be helping me deliver my baby. Her name was Tina, a newly qualified midwife, who would be supported by a more senior midwife. She was lovely and immediately put me at ease. Both my parents and the father were allowed in the room with me. I was supposed to write one of those 'birthing plan' things but never realised we would be in this position to need it at 30 weeks. I still had two drips in my arm, one with fluids and the other with the strep B antibiotics, hoping to fight the infection and protect my baby from contracting it.

12:30 pm - In went a third cannula for my drug-induced labour SYNTO drip, nicknamed baby jungle juice. This stuff was going to start my labour and fast. Funnily I sat there waiting for 'something' to happen quickly and was slightly disappointed that after five minutes, I felt nothing. "It may take a few hours to kick in."

12:40 pm- OUCH! Here it comes, my first contraction had hit, and my god it took my breath away! I was dripped up and attached to a monitor where I could watch each contraction come and go. They hit pretty hard and pretty fast. I had planned to navigate my labour with minimal pain relief, but this bloody hurt. I started on the gas and air which worked GREAT but gave me the giggles, which I supposed wasn't a bad thing after the disastrous couple of weeks I'd had. My midwife stayed in my room with me at all times and was a great comfort and support.

3:00 pm - "I'm just going to measure you and see how far you have dilated'. At this point, my contractions were coming hard and fast every 3-5 Mins so I must be doing pretty good. "3cm????" Are you bloody kidding me? 3 Minuscule CM? MY GOD, I need stronger pain medication. I was then offered a shot of pethidine or the option of an epidural. If I am ONLY 3cm with another 7 to go, I NEED an epidural. The frequency and strength of my contractions were just breathtaking.

3:50 pm - The Anaesthetist arrived to administer the epidural. "Now, when I have the needle in your spine, you MUST stay still". How the **** do you stay still when contractions are hitting you like bricks? It was a tense 30 minutes, as my contractions were still coming thick and fast. My parents had left, to pop to the cafe as my dad really struggled seeing me in so much pain.

4:30 pm - The epidural was complete, but I could still feel every inch of every contraction and had a sudden urge to push. "Tina, I need to push!" "Just hold on Lisa, I will measure you again, to see how much more you have dilated." I can remember just one thing, Tina had one glove on and then the unexpected happened.

4:40 pm - It seemed like a scene from 'Carry on Doctor' as the room was suddenly FULL of doctors. I was indeed, fully dilated and Dylan shot out like a tornado onto the bed, whilst Tina stood there with one glove on her hand. I remember the utter shock and panic on her face as she scrambled to catch the baby. It all happened so incredibly fast. At 3 pm I was only 3cm dilated, so in such a short space of time, I had dilated to 10cm before the epidural had time to set in. The Doctors took the baby straight away, with me shouting "What it the sex?" After what felt like forever, we heard a small cry, and my beautiful baby was placed in my arms and we were introduced to our beautiful little baby BOY. He had a mop of black hair and was absolutely Tiny at only 4lbs 2oz and just over ten weeks premature. But he was PERFECT!

Free bed and board at the hospital

We had doctors everywhere, and an incubator ready for my little boy to be taken to the special care baby unit. We had decided on a boy's name, and he was definitely a Dylan, the name just suited him. I led there crying that my baby boy had to be whisked away and needed to concentrate on getting my placenta out. This was another task that really didn't go to plan! I was still contracting to get it out, but it just did NOT want to budge. "On your next contraction Lisa, you push and I will pull the umbilical cord... Ready, Steady?" The next word "Oooooooooops" was not exactly what I needed to hear. The cord had snapped in the doctor's hand with no placenta attached. "Sorry Lisa but you will have to go up to the theatre for us to remove the placenta." How much more could go wrong? I felt like I was dreaming, with everything happening so fast.

Mum and Dad went up to see Dylan in special care and came back with a small photograph the nurses had taken of him in his incubator. Not having him with me, broke my heart but I knew he had to be checked over and antibiotics administered to protect him from the STREP B infection. I was still hooked up to drips and doctors checked my epidural in preparation for going to the theatre. I had a two-hour wait, as emergencies had come in, which took priority. I just ached to see my little baby boy and wanted this part of my nightmare over with as quickly as possible.

I was wheeled out of surgery, greeted by Dylans father with, "I'm gonna shoot off now, because I'm tired'. I had been through the mill, but he was TIRED. We hadn't even spent any time with Dylan, together, but I was way too tired and emotional to discuss it. I was wheeled up to SCBU intensive care on my hospital bed, to properly meet my baby, alone! It broke my heart, but the moment I laid eyes on him, my instinct kicked in, and I knew instantly that I would be his protector and loved him more than any words could describe. I was introduced to my nurse, who was there for me, and even hugged me when she could see how emotional I was. The sound of machines beeping was very Erie, amongst what felt like complete silence. I spent until the early hours, just sitting there, watching him and crying. Unfortunately I couldn't hold him, just put my hand through a side of the incubator. I needed to rest, after a pretty hectic day, so I was wheeled back to the ward, where I was greeted by three other mums, all with their babies. I didn't sleep a wink and spent most of the evening very emotional as MY baby wasn't with me.

The following day, I woke pretty early to get down to the special care unit as soon as I could. Just seeing Dylan again, was the most magical experience ever. He looked so tiny in his incubator but was snuggled up and sleeping so peacefully. He had had a good night, despite being wired up to machines and having blood taken every half an hour to check for infection. His poor little foot, was blue, from the needle pricks to take the blood. BUT, he was just perfect! I placed my hand inside the incubator and felt so much love and connection to this beautiful little boy.

Over the next two days, I was back and forth between the special care unit spending hours watching my little boy make slow but steady progress, then day three hit. I had a call from one of the SCBU nurses to say that I was needed as soon as possible. My heart was in my mouth going down in the lift, as I had no idea what could be the problem. I can remember running down the corridor into intensive care to be greeted by my nurse "Don't panic, there's nothing wrong he just won't settle and he needs his mummy! We've decided he needs a proper hug, so sit down get yourself comfortable and he's coming out of the incubator for his first cuddle." My heart was still in my mouth but for a very different reason than my initial thoughts. I will remember this moment forever, as even though he was still attached to all the machines, the nurses handed me this tiny little human and placed him in my arms.

I cried buckets but that feeling was like nothing I had ever experienced. I sat there kissing him, holding him as tight as possible and just looking at him in disbelief that he was actually here and in my arms. My god, he was perfect and beautiful! I spent nearly 2 hours sitting there until the very early hours of the morning. "It's time for you both to get some sleep!" So it was time to kiss the little man goodnight and head back onto the ward.

The design of the special care baby unit was genius. All

babies who needed intensive care started in there, then moved into cots in separate nurseries. Each baby would progress from intensive care, nursery one, nursery two, nursery three, nursery four then out the door. It gave us parents a clear pathway to getting home. Over the next three weeks, Dylan managed to get out of intensive as soon as his blood results were clear, and he progressed once his feeding was established. Initially, he was tube-fed, but with lots of support from the staff we moved on to breastfeeding. This was just beautiful and helped me bond even further with my little fella. I would very often feed him doing what they called 'Kangaroo care.' which was skin to skin, to help with our connection.

Our move to nursery four was very exciting, as I could see we were very close to getting home. After weeks of refusing to go home I was asked if I wanted to stay in the separate flat attached to the unit, where staff were still on hand to help me, but Dylan was finally out of the incubator and in a cot by the side of my bed. We were ready to head home, and I could not wait to start our life together as a family.

Find my full story on a journey of becoming a single parent, and discovering Dylan has autism in my up-and-coming book, 'Along came Dylan.'

You can connect with Lisa:

Facebook: www.facebook.com/lisanutland

"JUST A MUM TRYING TO NAVIGATE LIFE
THROUGH A VERY UNUSUAL PREGNANCY,
SINGLE PARENTING AND DISCOVERING
THAT MY PRECIOUS LITTLE BOY HAD
EARLY SIGNS OF ADDITIONAL NEEDS.
LIFE HAS HAD MANY UP'S AND DOWNS
FOR US, BUT LOVE AND STRENGTH
ALWAYS GOT US THROUGH!"

Lisa Nutland

GRIT AND GRACE

CHAPTER 9
BY NEZHA AIT AKKA

I started working when I was a teenager to buy lipsticks and fashion magazines, but my parents started working when they were children to buy food and to help in the family home.

I was born in a small remote village in the Atlas Mountains in Morocco. Life was hard, and child labour in the 1970s was the norm. I saw my parents working all the time; feeding children and having a roof over their heads was their only purpose. Back then, owning a car, going on holidays, or having fancy things didn't matter. If parents could feed their children every day, they were considered fortunate in our village. A full plate of our traditional couscous or a warm bowl of harira (soup) wasn't something every family could afford.

The women of the village would often share what little they had, sending their children with small portions of bread or dates to neighbours who they knew were struggling. Those who owned a cow or a few chickens were considered wealthy by village standards; their children at least had access to milk or eggs. The Tuesday-only local souk (market) was kilometres away, and many families could only afford to make the journey occasionally, carefully rationing their purchases until the next trip.

My parents, both incredibly hardworking, led by example. They showed us daily that nothing in life comes without effort and that hard work is the foundation for achieving anything meaningful. In our family, contributing to the household was seen not only as a duty but as a measure of a life well-lived.

I studied fashion and clothing design with dreams of becoming a designer. I was full of passion, but I didn't yet have the grit to match it. It took me years to realise that passion alone isn't enough to build a sustainable career; it requires effort, consistency, and resilience.

Back then, I struggled. I had grand visions of success, dreaming of becoming a designer overnight, but I didn't understand the level of work required to make those dreams a reality. My mindset was unstable, and I battled severe anxiety and panic attacks. Each setback felt overwhelming, and giving up on my projects seemed far easier than pushing through the challenges to make them work. Eventually, I let go of that passion entirely.

I moved on, working in Paris, Marbella, and London, taking on various roles—some lasting only briefly, others for longer periods. These experiences taught me about adaptability and perseverance, even if I didn't fully realise it at the time.

I felt like something was missing for many years. For me, grit and passion always felt out of sync. Passion would ignite briefly, but without the persistence to sustain it, my goals remained out of reach. But grit has a way of growing, often through life's demands and responsibilities. It didn't arrive all at once but built slowly, shaped by the experiences and challenges I faced. Looking back, I see how every failure, every struggle, and every restart helped me develop the resilience I needed to keep moving forward.

Like my parents, who had the courage to leave their land and family behind several times throughout their lives—moving from village to village and eventually immigrating from North Africa to Europe—I too embraced the bravery to try new things without always fearing what might go wrong. I am glad I inherited their adventurous nomad spirit in some ways.

I always felt inclined to be a businesswoman, maybe because my mom inspired me as she was a businesswoman and still is at over 80 years old. I remember she used to sell carpets in the local market when I was 5 or 6 years old.

I remember how she used to make carpets! In our home, weaving carpets was both art and tradition. My mother began with sheep's wool, washing and spinning it by hand before dyeing it with colours drawn from nature—saffron yellows, clay reds, and plant greens.

At her loom, she wove each knot with meticulous care, crafting patterns rich with symbolism—diamonds for protection, zigzags for strength. Every thread held meaning, and every carpet was a vivid reflection of our Amazigh heritage. I remember her teaching me how to weave, guiding my little hands with precision as she showed me the art of creating these intricate designs. In our quiet Moroccan village, far from the noise of the outside world, her work was more than just a craft; it was art, deeply rooted in culture and resilience. Once completed, the carpets were carefully washed, laid out under the sun to dry, and transformed into vibrant storytellers. Each piece, woven with skill, patience, and love, carried the essence of our heritage, ready to share its tale with the world.

She is the kind of person who can make something out of anything. She was and still is my role model!

Grace Under Pressure: Balancing Motherhood and Ambition

In 2005, my daughter was born. With now three young children, the only option for me was to work from home, set up my own business, and take care of my kids. I was determined to be there for them, to raise them, support them, and stay present in their lives. As a single parent, it was clear that leaving them with someone else and only seeing them for a few hours a day wasn't an option. Starting a home-based business became the perfect solution—and looking back, it was the best decision I ever made.

I was still working in our family business until it became too much to handle with school runs, pickups, homework, and kids' activities. In 2009, life changed altogether; I met someone who introduced me to my current business, and I jumped on the opportunity straight away! My three children were then 4, 8, and 12 years old.

What I didn't realise at the time was just how hard it would be to start and grow a business while raising three little children—two of whom had learning difficulties. Anyone who has ever built a business knows how challenging it is. Now imagine doing that while single-handedly raising three kids, with two being neurodivergent. It was overwhelming at times, but I was deeply committed to being there for my children, no matter what.

I'm proud to say I never missed a school trip, an assembly, a parent-teacher meeting, or a sick day when they needed to stay home. I was there for them, 100% of the time.

The biggest challenge of growing a business while raising young children is time. When you don't have kids, you can pour all your focus and energy into building the business. But when you're a single parent, you're constantly splitting your time—doubling up on parenting responsibilities and business tasks.

It's nonstop. You're working every day to grow the business, and at the same time, you're raising your kids every day without a break. I'll be honest, it was messy at the beginning. Really messy.

But I believe we learn and grow from every challenge, and over time, I found ways to organise, plan, and create systems that made life easier. Now, over 15 years later, I can confidently say it was all worth it.

Midnight Hustles and Morning Routines: Turning Chaos into Success

Raising children is a full-time job by itself; growing a business is a full-time job too. For as long as I remember, I had long days, weeks of marketing my business and looking for new clients while running school runs, helping with homework, and managing all that it takes to look after children. It always felt busy in our home! I often felt like a headless chicken, juggling business and home activities!

When you're running a business and raising kids, planning isn't just helpful—it's essential! I quickly learned that organisation was my lifeline. My kids' activities had to be planned and scheduled well in advance because juggling business tasks and parenting duties meant there was no room for last-minute chaos. Would you believe me if I told you that even with all the planning in the world, we had last-minute chaos? I'm sure that if you grew a business and kids at the same time, you'd agree!

From school drop-offs and pickups to sports practices, playdates, and doctor's appointments, everything had to be mapped out carefully. I kept detailed calendars, set reminders, and even colour-coded schedules to stay on top of things.

But it wasn't just about managing time; it was about being fully present. I didn't want my kids to ever feel like my work came before them, so I made it a priority to plan my day around their needs, ensuring I could be there for every important moment in their lives. Beyond that, I also needed to create a sense of security and stability for them, especially after the separation from their dad. It was essential that they felt safe, loved, and supported, no matter what.

At the same time, I had to carve out space for my business. Whether it was waking up before the children, working during nap times, or staying up late after bedtime, I found ways to fit it all in without sacrificing too much time with my children.

It wasn't always easy; there were days when I felt stretched too thin or worried, I was falling short in one area or another. But looking back, those carefully planned schedules helped me create a balance that allowed both my family and my business to thrive.

From Tears to Triumph: Overcoming Setbacks with Resilience

We've been taught to go to school, get a degree, and then find a job for life. For many, this linear path seems like the only viable option, a secure formula for success. But this way has not worked for me at all. Perhaps it's because I've always known, from past experiences, that we can create a fulfilling and prosperous life for ourselves without strictly following what society has prescribed. My journey taught me that setbacks are not the end of the road but rather opportunities to pivot and discover new possibilities.

What if everyone has an entrepreneurial mindset hidden within them, waiting to be unleashed? Many people never act on it, confined by fear, doubt, or societal expectations. Hear me out: why is it that so many entrepreneurs would never dream of adhering to the "normal" or "traditional" way? Why do they take the risks of setting up their own businesses, carving paths that seem unconventional or even risky? I believe it's because they've discovered their passion, followed their dreams, and summoned the grit to overcome challenges along the way. They dared to believe in a way of life that works for them, not one dictated by societal norms.

Now, imagine if we reimagined education. What if, instead of solely teaching the traditional model of degrees and job security, we encouraged students to explore their passions and equipped them with the tools to pursue their goals? What if resilience and creativity were emphasized as much as math and science? Imagine classrooms where children learn to identify their unique talents and interests, where they're taught how to set goals, face challenges head-on, and turn failures into stepping stones.

Certainly, some students would still choose the traditional path, earning degrees and securing careers as doctors, surgeons, judges, lawyers, accountants, scientists, engineers, or teachers among so many others. These professions are vital, and the traditional path is necessary for such roles. But what about all the other vocations that don't require a formal degree? What about those who dream of owning businesses, launching creative projects, creating their own products, or forging unique careers?

I didn't follow the conventional route. I earned a professional baccalaureate in my early twenties and later pursued certifications that aligned with my aspirations. My path was far from linear, but every obstacle I encountered became a stepping stone. Each challenge taught me resilience, determination, and adaptability. These traits became the foundation for my unique little business, and they are lessons I hope to pass on to others.

The truth is setbacks are inevitable. They're an integral part of life and growth. But setbacks don't define us; our response to them does. By embracing resilience and daring to dream beyond societal expectations, we can turn our tears into triumphs. We can create lives that are not only successful but also deeply fulfilling.

Leading by Example: Raising Strong, Independent Children

Building my business has been a transformative journey that's shaped not just my life but my children's perspectives in ways I never expected. As they've watched me build something from the ground up, they've absorbed invaluable lessons about perseverance, creativity, and the courage to pursue one's dreams.

From the beginning, I made it a point to be open with my children about both the challenges and triumphs of entrepreneurship. They've seen the reality of late nights at my desk, witnessed the excitement of successful projects, and understood the disappointment of setbacks.

These experiences have taught them that success isn't handed to anyone—it's earned through dedication and hard work.

What's been most rewarding is seeing how these lessons have naturally influenced their own approach to life. When my son was ten, he took the initiative to organise and run his very first-yard sale, demonstrating remarkable business sense for his age. He carefully sorted through his old toys, video games, and DVDs, researched their prices, made the display, and opened the door to get passersby's attention for sales! He learned to talk and negotiate with customers! This wasn't just about making pocket money—it was his first taste of entrepreneurship, and he embraced every aspect of it.

My daughter discovered her own entrepreneurial spirit through creating and selling slime in primary school. What started as a fun hobby evolved into a small business, with her selling her creations to schoolmates and at local fairs. She learned to perfect her product, handle customer feedback, and manage her earnings. When batches didn't turn out right, she showed remarkable resilience, adjusting her formula until she got it just right.

These experiences have taught my children valuable lessons about adaptability and problem-solving. They've learned that setbacks aren't failures but opportunities to learn and improve. More importantly, they've developed a strong sense of independence and confidence in their abilities to create something of their own.

Leading by example has become one of the most meaningful aspects of my entrepreneurial journey. Beyond building a successful business, I've had the privilege of raising children who understand the value of hard work, resilience, and self-reliance. Watching them take initiative and pursue their own projects with enthusiasm shows me that they're developing the mindset and skills they'll need to achieve their future goals.

As they continue to grow, I hope these early experiences will serve as a foundation for their future endeavours. They're learning that with determination, creativity, and perseverance, they can overcome challenges and turn their ideas into reality. This might be my most important legacy: raising children who believe in themselves and their ability to shape their own path in life.

Dreams Don't Wait: Building a Legacy of Strength and Success

Success in business is often measured in profits and growth, but the true measure of success extends far beyond financial statements. As I've built my business and raised my children simultaneously, I've come to understand that the legacy we create isn't just about the enterprises we build; it's about the values, mindset, and inspiration we pass on to the next generation.

Looking back at my entrepreneurial journey, I realise that every challenge I faced was an opportunity to demonstrate important life lessons to my children. When I chose to start my business despite the uncertainties, I showed them that dreams don't wait for perfect timing. When I persevered through difficult periods, I taught them that resilience isn't just about surviving; it's about emerging stronger.

One of the most profound realisations I've had is that pursuing your dreams and nurturing family values aren't mutually exclusive goals. In fact, they can reinforce each other in powerful ways. By involving my children in age-appropriate aspects of my business journey, I've helped them develop a strong work ethic while maintaining our close family bonds. Those moments when we brainstormed ideas together at the dinner table or celebrated small victories as a family became the building blocks of their entrepreneurial mindset.

The impact of this approach became clear as I watched my children develop their own initiatives. Their confidence in pursuing their ideas, whether it's a yard sale or a slime business, stems from seeing that success is achievable through dedication and hard work. They've learned that setbacks are natural stepping stones on the path to achievement, not roadblocks that should deter them from their goals.

But perhaps the most valuable legacy I'm building is showing them that success doesn't require sacrificing your values or family relationships. By maintaining open communication, setting boundaries, and making time for family despite business demands, I've demonstrated that it's possible to build something meaningful while staying true to what matters most.

This journey has taught me that building a legacy isn't about choosing between being a successful entrepreneur or a present parent; it's about integrating both roles in a way that enriches everyone involved. When my children see me negotiate deals with integrity, treat clients with respect, and maintain work-life boundaries, they're learning lessons that will serve them well beyond any business success.

As I look to the future, my hope is that this legacy extends beyond my immediate family. I want to inspire other parents, especially mothers, to pursue their entrepreneurial dreams without guilt. Your journey might look different from others, and that's okay. What matters is staying true to your values while showing your children that with passion, perseverance, and purpose, dreams are achievable.

To those reading this who are hesitating to take that first step toward their dreams: remember that your children are watching and learning from your example. By pursuing your goals with determination and integrity, you're teaching them invaluable lessons about courage, resilience, and the importance of staying true to oneself.

The legacy we build isn't just in the businesses we create or the wealth we accumulate; it's in the values we instil, the examples we set, and the courage we inspire in others to pursue their own dreams. When we lead with purpose and stay true to our values, we create a ripple effect that influences not just our children, but generations to come.

Let your journey be a testament to the fact that dreams don't wait, and success doesn't have to come at the expense of what matters most. Build your legacy with intention, knowing that every step you take forward paves the way for those who follow. After all, the greatest success story isn't just about achieving our own dreams; it's about inspiring others to pursue theirs.

My children are now 19 (soon to be 20), 23, and 27. They've boldly pursued their dreams, ones they've longed for since childhood. With grit, passion, and resilience, they've carved their own paths. And I, as a single mumpreneur, have embraced every challenge, fulfilled my purpose, and witnessed their growth into remarkable individuals. Together, we've created a story of perseverance, love, and success.

Ready to Start Your Mompreneur Journey?

Are you a mother dreaming of building a business while being present for your children? I understand the unique challenges you face, and I'm here to help. With over 15 years of experience balancing entrepreneurship and motherhood, I offer personalised mentoring to help you:

- Create a business that works around your family life
- Develop systems to manage your time effectively
- Build confidence in your entrepreneurial abilities
- Navigate the challenges of being a mompreneur
- Turn your passion into a sustainable business

Let's work together to transform your dreams into reality. Your children are watching, and your success will inspire them to pursue their own dreams.

Connect with me at and begin Your Mompreneur journey here! **To your success, Nezha Ait Akka**

My profile webpage: www.one2onediet.com/Nezha

Facebook: https://www.facebook.com/nezhacambridge1/

Instagram: www.instagram.com/nezhacambridge/

Telegram: https://t.me/Nezhaone2oneDietInLondon

My business on Google: Nezha one2one diet consultant

LinkedIn: www.linkedin.com/in/nezhaone2onediet-by-cambridgeweightplan

"WHEN THE WORLD SAID 'IMPOSSIBLE',
I WAS TOO BUSY BEING A MOM AND
AN ENTREPRENEUR TO LISTEN."

Nezha Ait Akka!

GRIT AND GRACE

CHAPTER 10
My journey through struggle, self-discovery & success

BY SAMANTHA THISTLETHWAITE

A hug for the little girl who didn't know

If I could go back and hug the little girl who felt everything so deeply, who struggled to understand why she felt different, I would. If I could sit beside teenage me, the girl who fought silent battles with food, emotions, and self-worth, I would tell her, you are not broken. You are not wrong. You are just wired differently, and one day, you'll see how powerful that is.

I didn't know then what I know now. At 37 years old, my ADHD diagnosis made my entire life make sense. The struggles, the inconsistencies, the rollercoaster of emotions, the feeling of being "too much" or "not enough".... It was all part of something bigger. Something that explained the chaos but also the grit that kept me pushing forward and building a life I could have only dreamed of.

Now, I run a successful cleaning business, I have built a community of 12,000 cleaners across the UK, and I coach business owners to find their own success. I've fought battles against self-doubt, medical gaslighting, endometriosis, surgical menopause, and a mind that never quite knew how to switch off. But I came through it all, not just surviving, but thriving.

This is my story. A story of resilience, of learning to embrace who I am, and of finding glamour in the grit.

The busy bee that felt too much

From the outside, I looked like any other little girl, chatty, full of energy, and always on the move. But inside, I was a storm of emotions I didn't understand. Jealousy, sadness, frustration, excitement, and everything felt bigger to me than it seemed to other kids. Adults called me a 'busy bee,' but I never felt busy, I felt restless.

In primary school, I was often alone in a room full of people and I struggled to fit in. I watched other kids build easy friendships, while I felt like an outsider even when I was included. Why did I feel different? I didn't have the words for it then, but I knew I wasn't like everyone else.

And the emotions, oh, the emotions. I cried easily, I loved hard, and I felt things deeper than I knew how to handle. One minute, I was on top of the world; the next, I felt invisible. But no one ever asked why. They just saw a sensitive, overdramatic little girl who couldn't control herself.

The battle with my own reflection

As a teenager, those emotions turned inward. Anorexia, bulimia, and self-hate. I didn't just struggle with my emotions anymore; I struggled with myself. My self-image was warped, and my need for control was overwhelming. If I could control my body, maybe I could control the chaos in my mind.

I spent years trapped in that cycle, starving, binging, punishing, and hiding. I never told anyone how bad it got. On the outside, I kept up appearances. But on the inside, I was breaking. And then, as I hit my going-out years, I traded one coping mechanism for another, alcohol. Drinking gave me an escape, a way to turn off the noise in my head. But it also made me wild, unpredictable, and reckless. I was the life of the party until I wasn't. I drank to blackout, to silence the thoughts that never stopped.

Love, stability & the next chapter

Meeting my now husband changed things. For the first time, I felt grounded, he was in the military, and our life together started fast, two kids, a husband away on deployments, and me juggling everything alone. But I never stopped moving, never stopped chasing something more.

I tried everything, jobs around the kids, network marketing, side hustles. I could never settle, never just 'be.' friends came and went, relationships were strained, because one day I was one Sam, the next I was another Sam. I was too much, too emotional, too inconsistent. I didn't understand why I was like this, but I knew one thing, I wanted more in life.

The move that changed everything

When we moved to Gibraltar, it was the best two years of my life. The sun, the sea, the freedom, I felt alive. I exercised every day, ran everywhere, burned off the energy that never left me. But looking back, I see it now, the erratic thoughts, the restless energy, the highs and lows. I didn't know then that this was part of something bigger.

The hardest battle – endometriosis & menopause

Then came the worst fight of all endometriosis. Years of pain, doctors dismissing me, hormones wreaking havoc, medical menopause, surgical menopause, and with it, my mental health spiralled.

It was the turning point. My mind was all over the place, worse than it had ever been. Something was wrong, but it wasn't just menopause, and that's when I finally got the answer that changed everything.

The ADHD diagnosis that made my life make sense

At 37, I was diagnosed with ADHD, and suddenly, everything made sense. The rollercoaster emotions. the inconsistencies. the restlessness. The struggles with self-control, focus, and friendships. I wasn't broken, I wasn't lazy, I wasn't just "too much."

I had ADHD and no one had ever seen it.

As I learned more, I realised I wasn't alone. So many women, especially those diagnosed late, had been through the same thing. We'd spent our whole lives thinking we were the problem, only to find out that our brains just worked differently. And with that knowledge came power. Building my best life – business, success & helping others armed with understanding, I took control.

I built my cleaning company. I found my passion in helping others. I created a community of 12,000 cleaners across the UK, coaching them, mentoring them, and guiding them. And now? I'm living my best life.

I still have good days and bad. ADHD never goes away, but I understand myself now. I know how to work with my brain, not against it. I know that grit got me here, and glamour followed. And if my story helps just one person feel less alone, less broken, and more seen, then every struggle was worth it.

Final thoughts: From chaos to clarity

To the little girl who felt lost, to the teenager who battled her body, to the woman who never felt enough—I see you now. and I'm proud of you. Because you made it, we made it, and this? This is just the beginning.

Contact Samantha:
Facebook: Samantha Thistlethwaite

GRIT AND GRACE

"SHE FOUGHT A BATTLE NO ONE COULD
SEE, CARRIED EMOTIONS TOO HEAVY TO
HOLD, AND ONLY LATER REALISED THE
POWER IN UNDERSTANDING HERSELF.
THAT'S WHERE HER HEALING BEGAN."

Samantha Thistlethwaite

GRIT AND GRACE

CHAPTER 11
BY SARAH LAYLA REID

Angry voices & borderline personality disorder

“ *You're useless*!” The words echoed in my head, sharp and merciless, slicing through my thoughts like a knife cutting through butter. They burned with the kind of anger that seemed to come from nowhere, the kind that could easily drown me. Another seizure today—this one, came out of nowhere, after a whole year of being seizure-free. That moment made me realise that, yet another year would pass before I could even think about getting my driving licence back. My independence, that tiny flicker of hope that had been growing, was extinguished in an instant.

Excitement had once filled my mind like a sudden bolt of lightning. The plan was simple: Tomorrow, I would go to the post office and pick up an application to reapply for my driving licence. The dream of driving again, of regaining control over my life, seemed within my grasp. after two long years, I would no longer be dependent on my family to drive me to work or run errands. But that moment of anticipation was shattered in the blink of an eye.

Out of nowhere, the seizure struck. My legs gave way as I staggered across the living room like a newborn foal, struggling to stay upright. And then, without warning, I collapsed, shaking uncontrollably. The fall was heavy, my body collapsing onto the sofa like a sack of potatoes. I had never had alcohol in my life, but in that moment, I looked drunk, disoriented, and confused. The memory of a man yelling at me in the supermarket months ago flooded back. He had assumed I was drunk, his angry words echoing in my mind.

Tears began to stream down my face, as heavy as the storm clouds gathering overhead. Phoebe, the cat, came to me, sensing my distress. her rough, sandpaper-like tongue gently licked my nose, her presence a small comfort as I lay on the sofa, exhausted and broken. I felt heavy, shattered—like a broken doll with no strings left to hold me up.

Why had this happened again, after so long? Why did this seizure have to strike now, when I had finally dared to hope? I was tired, emotionally drained, and tearful. The weight of another year ahead of relying on others, of needing lifts to appointments and shopping, weighed on me like an anchor.

Using public transport was becoming increasingly difficult, too. The buses were unreliable, and often late, and I had grown accustomed to the judgmental stares I received when I showed my disabled bus pass. "You don't look disabled," they would silently accuse, as though I needed to explain my epilepsy to every person I encountered.

As I reflected on the past week, the sheer number of stressors came into focus. Financial worries hung over me like a storm cloud, and the red letters from the bank warning of my nearing overdraft limit seemed to scream at me. Exhaustion from double shifts at work added to the growing weight on my shoulders. My mind felt like it was spinning out of control, with the triggers for my seizure building up one after another, like an avalanche waiting to bury me.

Reality crashed down hard, and the tears flowed again. The voices in my head screamed, "*you're useless*!" like thunder in a storm. The anger was consuming me, the frustration too much to bear. I staggered through the hallway, visions of jeering faces swirling in my mind as my body felt drained and lifeless. I stumbled into the kitchen, my eyes landing on the knife block. In that moment, the urge was overwhelming. I yanked a knife from the block and pulled up my sleeve. The blade sliced across my wrist in one swift motion, and I felt a strange sense of relief as the pain washed over me, distracting from the suffocating anger that gripped me.

The blood trickled down my wrist slowly, like a snake winding through the grass, and for a brief moment, I felt lighter. The tension in my shoulders eased, the pressure lifting, but it was only temporary. As soon as I heard my daughter come home from school, I quickly pulled down my sleeves and pretended nothing was wrong. I forced a smile, hiding the pain that was coursing through me as if everything was fine.

"How was your day at school?" I asked, my voice bright, but hollow. inside, I was falling apart. She threw her satchel onto the chair, mumbling a response before retreating to the living room, eyes glued to her phone. I returned to the kitchen, quietly opening the cupboard to find the first aid kit. My hands trembled as I wrapped the wound, hoping she wouldn't notice.

Going out was always a battle, even the simplest of tasks—touching door handles, entering a shop, or using a cash machine—triggered intrusive thoughts and compulsions. "*You're a failure!*" the voices would scream at me, "*The world would be better off without you.*" Every interaction felt like a judgement. Every glance, a silent accusation. I was convinced everyone was watching me, scrutinising me, thinking I was worthless.

I could never walk down the street without feeling like I was being judged. Every person I passed, from the elderly woman with the squeaky shopping trolley to the frail man sitting on a rusty bench smoking his cigar, became a silent witness to my inner turmoil. The voices echoed louder, mocking me, calling me "fat" or "crazy." The anger bubbled up again, but so did the exhaustion. It became too much. I fled home, my heart racing, and tears streaking down my face.

"Why can't I even walk to the shop without feeling like I'm drowning in these voices?" I asked myself in frustration. But the anger was fleeting. The exhaustion soon took over, and I collapsed, falling asleep on the sofa. The seventeen pills I took every day, trying to manage my multiple health conditions, left me in a fog, confused and drained.

When my family noticed the weight loss, the restricted eating, and the constant exercising, they pushed me to see the doctor. Sitting in the sterile white room, I felt like I was suffocating. The doctor's smile was warm, but I couldn't bring myself to meet his eyes. My gaze was fixed on the floor, heart pounding in my chest like a war drum.

"Do you have an eating disorder?" he asked gently.

I shook my head, denying it, though deep down, I knew the truth. I had been hiding the symptoms for so long. He asked about self-harm, about whether I was making myself sick. Again, I denied it, tugging my sleeves down to cover my scarred arms, desperately trying to hide the truth.

When he asked to take my blood pressure, my nerves spiked, and I reluctantly pulled up my sleeve just far enough to avoid showing the deep, jagged scars on my arms. He gently coaxed me to roll my sleeve up further, and with a flush of shame, I complied. When he saw the evidence, he sat quietly for a moment before asking me how it had happened.

That was when it all came crashing down. The floodgates opened, and everything poured out in a tidal wave of emotion. My anger, my frustration, my sense of hopelessness—it all spilled over, and I found myself speaking out loud for the first time in what felt like forever. The doctor listened patiently, and I was referred for counselling and given antidepressants.

Slowly, as the weeks passed, I felt a small shift, a glimmer of hope.

But even then, the feeling of being trapped didn't leave me. The four walls of my room felt suffocating, the dusty pictures on the shelves glaring at me as though they were witnesses to my pain. Charlie, my sister's dog, sensed my restlessness and came to me, his rough fur brushing against my leg. Despite the overwhelming urges from my OCD and BPD to resist, I grabbed his lead and walked with him outside.

But just as I began to feel a brief sense of relief, a seizure hit me once more, and I staggered, feeling disoriented, unable to control my body. Charlie sensed something was wrong and guided me back home, as confusion and fear washed over me like a tidal wave.

It seemed like every step forward was followed by two steps back, and yet, somehow, I kept going.

The Struggles Within: Seizures, Stigma, and Isolation

As Charlie guided me carefully up the path, his sharp howl pierced the quiet, a desperate signal to my dad that something was terribly wrong. His shrill cry was full of panic, a cry that seemed to echo through the chilly air, desperate for help. In a stroke of luck, dad had just woken from a much-needed cat nap. After long, exhausting night shifts, his body was always fighting against the relentless tide of exhaustion, and he needed every minute of sleep he could get.

He heard Charlie's call and glanced up from the ornaments lined up across the living room, his tired eyes scanning the surroundings. It didn't take long for him to notice me—staggering unsteadily up the path, my mind clouded in a thick, blurry haze of confusion. It was as though the world around me was slipping in and out of focus, leaving me disoriented, as if I were walking through a fog. I felt a strange sense of detachment, like I was floating rather than walking. Dad rushed to the door, opening it with a speed born of panic, and swiftly guided me into the house.

Once inside, he led me to the sofa, where I collapsed, my body heavy and broken. I felt like a rag doll being placed slumping on the cushions. I was so drained, my limbs feeling like lead. Charlie, sensing my distress, stayed close by, licking my hand with his rough, comforting tongue as if to say, "You're safe now." His presence felt grounding—his soft whimpering and comforting nudges reassured me that I wasn't alone in the chaos of my mind. He was there, guarding me.

As I slowly began to come around, the fuzziness in my mind started to lift. Dad had placed a cup of water on the table in front of me. The coolness of it was a welcome touch of reality amidst the disorienting blur of my thoughts. He didn't ask many questions—just quietly explained what had happened, his voice low and steady. His presence felt like a safety net, a reminder that even though everything inside me felt like it was crumbling, there were still people who cared enough to catch me when I fell.

I whispered my thanks to Charlie, my voice hoarse, as I gently stroked his fur. He was lying by my feet, eyes soft and watchful, his head raised in alertness, as if he knew the worst had passed but was still on guard for me. He was my protector. His whimpering continued, soft and reassuring, as if telling me that I was safe now, that I didn't have to face this alone.

The anger and frustration swirled inside me—tangled with gratitude. Why had this happened again? And yet, amidst the storm of emotions, I found comfort in the small things: Dad's soothing words, Charlie's presence, and the gentle sense of security that wrapped around me like a warm blanket.

Finding Strength: Therapy, Support, and Self Discovery

The journey ahead was uncertain, but I wasn't going to face it in isolation. I had the support of medical professionals, therapists, and a team of people who helped guide me through the storm. My neurologist, along with other specialists, had offered me a range of therapies and suggestions. For the next three and a half years, I worked tirelessly, testing out different techniques, adjusting my mindset, and trying new approaches. One of those therapies was a weekly visit to a mental health hospital, where I began to learn how to cope with my conditions.

One day, after a particularly gruelling session, I sat outside the hospital on a stone wall, waiting for my lift home. A woman jogged past me, her breathing heavy from the effort. She stopped when she saw me, a polite smile forming on her face as she caught her breath. I didn't recognize her at first, and panic began to well up inside me. My mind scrambled for an answer, trying to place her. and then, she spoke.

"Hi Sarah—haven't seen you in ages!"

Her words triggered a faint recognition. High school, I thought. A vague memory began to surface. I nodded and forced a polite smile, but inside, I was still lost, trying to connect the dots.

And then, as her gaze fell on the hospital sign, her expression changed. The warmth in her smile evaporated, replaced by an almost imperceptible look of shock. It was as if she'd seen something alarming, and in that moment, the stigma of mental health reared its ugly head. For years, the hospital had been the subject of cruel rumours—the kind that painted anyone associated with it as "crazy" or dangerous. She didn't even try to mask her discomfort. With a hurried excuse, she turned and jogged away, faster than before.

The shock of it hit me hard. Anger surged within me. How could anyone judge me—judge anyone—simply because they were receiving care for a mental health condition? Why should it be so shameful to admit that you need help? The sting of rejection was sharp, but it also ignited something within me—a deep, burning resolve. I would not be defined by the whispers of judgment. I would fight to change how people viewed those of us struggling with mental health.

In the years that followed, I was diagnosed with borderline personality disorder (BPD), an eating disorder, OCD, and depression. At first, the diagnosis terrified me. I had never heard of BPD, and the thought of being "locked away" in a facility filled me with dread. The voices in my head screamed that I was "crazy," that I would never recover, that I was a burden to those around me. But slowly, over time and through therapy, I started to regain my confidence. I learned to acknowledge the voices and not act on them, to let them be there without letting them control my actions.

With therapy, I found ways to cope—writing down my feelings in a journal, reaching out to friends for support, and learning how to challenge the destructive thoughts that clouded my mind. Each step felt like a victory, no matter how small. Gradually, my world expanded. I went from struggling to leave the house to walking short distances on my own, then taking trips to the local shop to buy milk without a therapist by my side.

The voices grew quieter over time, or at least, I learned to ignore them. Slowly, my confidence began to rebuild, and with that came a desire to share my story. I wanted others to know that they weren't alone—that they didn't have to face their struggles in isolation.

Turning Pain into Purpose: Advocacy, Awareness, and Empowerment

Writing about my experiences, and sharing my journey with others, became my therapy. It gave me a sense of purpose, a way to turn my pain into something meaningful. It also allowed me to raise awareness about epilepsy and mental health, to help break down the stigma that so many people with hidden disabilities face.

Over the years, I raised thousands of pounds for epilepsy charities and helped spread awareness through talks and community events. My daughter's book, which raised money for epilepsy research, became a symbol of hope for many. Despite the obstacles life threw at us, we kept pushing forward—one step at a time.

I've come a long way from the person who couldn't leave her home without overwhelming anxiety. Today, I continue to advocate for epilepsy awareness, mental health, and hidden disabilities. I've learned that despite the challenges, there is always a way forward. No matter how dark it may seem, there is always a glimmer of hope—just waiting to be discovered.

To support Sarah's charities go to:

https://www.crowdfunder.co.uk/p/epilepsy-information-packs-for-schools-2

GRIT AND GRACE

"GIVING ISN'T JUST ABOUT MAKING A
DONATION—IT'S ABOUT MAKING A
DIFFERENCE. PASSION FOR CHARITY IS
PASSION FOR CHANGE, FOR HOPE, AND
FOR A BETTER WORLD."

Sarah Layla Reid

GRIT AND GRACE

CHAPTER 12
Legacy in Motion

BY SKYLAR ACAMESIS

How I Went from Physical Broken to Building a Spiritual Empire

B reaking the Generational Money Mould Success was written into my lineage, but so was struggle. I come from a family that believed in the gospel of hard work—the kind that demands everything from you, that shapes your existence before you even know how to question it. On my father's side, excellence wasn't optional; it was an expectation. He immigrated from Brazil to Scotland when I was four years old, carrying with him the inheritance of a relentless work ethic and the unspoken rule that success must be earned through sacrifice.

My mother's side was no different. My grandmother was one of the first women in Rio to secure a divorce at a time when it was nearly unthinkable. She broke barriers again by earning her degree and establishing a powerful career, becoming a force in her own right. The message woven into my DNA was clear: if you want something, you work for it. No shortcuts. No excuses. And, most importantly, you must be better—better than others, better than circumstances, better than what society expects of you.

But with that inheritance came the weight of expectation. It wasn't just about success; it was about survival. Being an immigrant, a woman, and navigating the undercurrents of discrimination meant that excellence wasn't just encouraged—it was required. Failure wasn't an option, and neither was ease. The programming that shaped my childhood was that life would be hard, and I had to be willing to push harder.

Yet, beneath the drive for achievement, another narrative played out. When we left Brazil and moved to Scotland, financial struggles became part of our reality. My father was still studying, and my mother was supporting not just him but three young children. Despite some help from my grandparents, money was tight. I watched my mother stretch resources in impossible ways, often sacrificing her own well-being to ensure we had what we needed. I saw the exhaustion in her eyes, the way she put herself last, and somewhere along the way, I absorbed the message that financial success meant personal depletion.

That belief was a cage I had to break free from.

For years, I carried the unconscious programming that success and suffering were intertwined—that wealth demanded sacrifice, and that abundance came at the cost of freedom. It didn't matter how much I achieved; I was still running on the belief that working myself to the bone was the only way to get ahead. Even as I built a career, those patterns followed me, dictating my choices and limiting my potential.

Education was another battlefield. While my family had a strong belief in academia, I felt the pull toward something different—something unconventional, something beyond what a degree could provide. But the idea that income had to come from a formal qualification was deeply ingrained in my upbringing. It took years to unravel that belief, to realise that my worth wasn't tied to a piece of paper but to the impact and transformation I could create.

And then there was money itself. For a long time, I feared it. I had seen what it did to my family. I had watched my father work tirelessly, always chasing, never arriving. I had seen my mother sacrifice and struggle. And I had drawn the conclusion that money was the enemy—that it stole time, drained energy, and created more suffering than it solved.

But that was a lie.

I had to confront the distortion and unlearn the fear that had been programmed into me. Money was never the problem; the mindset around it was. It wasn't evil. It wasn't something to be avoided or feared. It was a magnifier—an amplifier of what was already within us.

And it was my responsibility to rewrite the narrative.

One of the most powerful lessons I ever received came from my mother. She told me, *"If you don't like what we've done as your parents, do better."* Those words became my compass. Whenever I was faced with a limiting belief, whenever I stood at the edge of a breakthrough but felt resistance, I asked myself: *Am I willing to do better?*

That question guided me through every leap of faith—starting not one business, but three. Learning to invest instead of just earning. Valuing myself instead of waiting for the world to do it for me.

Breaking free from those inherited limitations wasn't just about personal success. It was about something much bigger. I knew that my transformation wasn't just for me—it was for every woman who had been told she had to suffer for her success, for every person who had been taught to fear money, for every healer who had been conditioned to believe that their gift should be given away for free.

Stepping from grit to grace wasn't about luck. It was about burning down the false beliefs that had been passed down for generations and replacing them with truth. And the truth was this: abundance isn't something we chase. It's something we *allow*. It's something we *become*.

And the moment I truly understood that everything changed.

From Vision to Reality

The pivotal moment in my life wasn't a slow evolution—it was an explosion of understanding. My spiritual awakening changed everything. I realized, with a certainty that shook me, that I was the creator of my own experiences. I wasn't meant to just struggle through life. I was meant to lead, to teach, to heal.

I began receiving visions—clear, powerful glimpses of my future. I saw myself speaking to thousands, guiding people to heal themselves and others. I saw financial ease, and abundance flowing in ways that defied logic. I didn't know how it would happen, but I didn't need to. The message was clear: *trust the vision, follow the guidance, and let go of control.*

That's when my relationship with money shifted. I stopped seeing it as something earned through toil and sacrifice. Instead, I saw it as an extension of purpose—a divine resource, channelled to those who step into their higher calling. I learned to work for God, not just for survival.

This shift wasn't theoretical—it was immediate. A man came to me, homeless, with only five pounds for an angel reading. That single session healed the grief that had led him to the streets. Within months, he was back on his feet, reunited with his family, building wealth of his own. That's when I understood: transformation doesn't have to be hard. It doesn't have to take years. It can be instant, effortless—if we allow it. I started offering readings on abundance. People came to me for guidance on investments, business, and wealth—and they began seeing extraordinary results. Opportunities multiplied. My income grew. I no longer charged five or ten pounds for my work—I recognized its worth, and I treated it like the gold it was.

There were obstacles, of course. I battled my own limiting beliefs, the echoes of childhood conditioning telling me I had to *earn* success the hard way. But I knew that staying stuck in the old cycle—working to survive rather than thriving in purpose—was its own kind of suffering. I chose a different path.

And the universe responded.

Doors opened. Clients came. Financial freedom followed. But most importantly, I felt *alive*—completely, powerfully, unapologetically aligned with my purpose.
And this was only the beginning.

Building the Dream

My entrepreneurial journey really started with my angel readings, but it was catalysed by starting a company with my husband. I still remember him and his friend asking me if they should incorporate, and when I said yes, they invited me to join. That moment made me realize that I needed a company for my spiritual work, and for the first time, I began to see business not as something intimidating, but as an energetic container for creation.

I never thought of myself as a businesswoman. In school, I avoided anything remotely related to business or finance like the plague. I associated business with struggle, exhaustion, and soulless transactions. But that belief changed when I met my first spiritual mentor, Anna Kidney. Watching her teach Theta Healing and run a thriving company opened my eyes to something I had never considered—business could be spiritual, powerful, and deeply transformational.

She didn't just inspire me; she challenged me. She demanded that I raise my standards, take my business seriously, and stop treating my gifts as a hobby. She made me look at the financial trauma I had ignored, the ancestral fears I was still carrying, and the ways I had been playing small.

Then came COVID-19. The Theta Healing company I worked for shut down overnight, and suddenly, I had to build something of my own. People were dying. Healers and teachers were looking to me for guidance because I specialized in health. But I was also pregnant, and I couldn't put myself at risk. I had to find a way to serve, to create, to *receive*.

I had to get uncomfortable. I had to step fully into my own power.

That's when I received the vision for a virtual school—one that would not only teach people how to heal but would also fund real-world hospitals and schools. A school that couldn't be manipulated by external forces because it would be built on pure, unfiltered divine knowledge. The vision was bigger than health. It was about life itself.

I had spent years working in other people's businesses, learning from them, and supporting their dreams. But the moment came when I had to stop hiding in their shadow and build something of my own. The resistance was real. The fear was suffocating. But I refused to let it dictate my future.

So, I stepped forward. I booked rooms in London. I organized events. I put my name out there in ways I never thought I would. And I watched as everything I had been calling in— everything I had prayed for—began to manifest. I let go of control, trusted the divine timing, and moved with faith.

And that's exactly what changed everything.

Impact and Intuition

Today, at 36 years old, I own three six-figure companies that are rapidly growing. This success has not only provided me with financial security but has allowed me to maintain and expand my businesses while raising two beautiful sons—one of whom is just a year old. The ability to create and sustain thriving companies while being fully present for my family is something I never imagined possible, yet here I am, living it.

Beyond financial success, I have created not just one, but four distinct healing modalities. I am a best-selling author. My spiritual virtual school continues to expand, reaching students across the world and growing stronger every day. This means I can provide my children with a quality of life I could never have dreamed of, but even more importantly, I can give back to my community in meaningful ways.

Through free angel readings, scholarships, and extensive spiritual resources, I am committed to ensuring that powerful spiritual knowledge is accessible to those who need it most.

I actively mentor and support aspiring healers and spiritual teachers, helping them overcome their own barriers and step fully into their purpose. My focus is not just on healing but on creating leaders in the spiritual space.

The next step in my journey is the launch of **Seven Figure Psychic**, a program designed to help spiritual entrepreneurs achieve the same level of success and impact I have experienced. It is the culmination of everything I have learned—the principles, the mindset shifts, the business strategies that turn spiritual gifts into thriving businesses.

Ultimately, my mission extends far beyond personal success. My long-term vision is to establish **physical** healing centers and schools across the world—places where knowledge and healing are not controlled by outside forces but remain accessible and pure. My goal is to have at least one in every city, and in every country, creating a global network of transformative education and healing.

My success isn't just measured in income, businesses, or the number of students I've trained—it's measured in the **legacy I'm building**. I have built not just companies but an empire of transformation. My work has moved beyond the virtual space, beyond financial freedom, beyond personal ambition. I am here to **redefine wealth and healing on a global scale**.

The vision is clear: hospitals, schools, and institutions that belong to the people, not to corrupt systems. A **new paradigm of education and healing**, rooted in divine truth and self-empowerment, where no one is left behind. I am not just teaching people to make money—I am teaching them to own their power, reclaim their sovereignty, and rise as leaders.

But I cannot do this alone. This movement needs **visionaries, disruptors, healers, and spiritual entrepreneurs** who are ready to step up, to create their own wealth, and to claim their place in this transformation. If you have ever felt the call to **do more, be more, give more**—this is your moment.

The world doesn't change because we wait for permission. It changes because we **decide**. So, I ask you now: *Will you be a part of this re-creation? Will you choose to claim your power, rewrite your story, and create the impact you were born to make?*

The time is now. The path is open. **Step in. The future is waiting.**

Facebook: /skyacamesisInstagram: @skylaracamesis

Twitter: @skyacamesis

YouTube: /c/Skylar444

Telegram: https://t.me/+iQGzpg4NIOw0MTNk

https://linktr.ee/skylaracamesisFull

https://skyacamesis.thrivecart.com/seven-figure-psychic/

"THERE IS NO LIMIT TO WHAT WE, AS WOMEN, CAN ACCOMPLISH."

Michelle Obama

GRIT AND GRACE

CHAPTER 13

BY TRACEY MUNRO

From Multiple Successful Businesses to Best-Selling
Author Coaching—My Journey to Pro Publishing House

It's funny how life can sometimes take you on a path you never quite expected, but when you look back, it all makes perfect sense. I've been in business for over 30 years now, but my journey wasn't always straightforward. It was filled with twists, turns, lessons, and a whole lot of heart. And today, as I sit here reflecting on everything I've done—helping hundreds of female entrepreneurs, through business coaching and aspiring authors, to building successful product brands—I can't help but feel an overwhelming sense of gratitude for the roads I've walked.

Let's rewind a bit. The first big chapter of my business story began with a hotel! That's where I met my husband Chris, from there I opened several successful salons to network marketing. When I entered the world of network marketing, I had no idea what I was getting into, but what I did have was passion and a fierce drive to succeed. And it worked. Within the first year, my business grew to the point where it was turning over seven figures every year. That was a huge accomplishment, and it was also a massive learning experience.

But success in one area doesn't always mean staying in that same place forever. After a while, I realised I was ready for something new. It wasn't about leaving behind what I'd built— it was about expanding and diving into another area that truly excited me. I wanted to give back. I wanted to help others build their own businesses and create their own success stories. And then, the idea hit me: book coaching as well as business coaching!

You see, my husband and I had just finished writing our first book. It was a huge accomplishment, and one I'll always cherish. Writing that book sparked something in me— something I hadn't realised was missing. The entire process of putting our thoughts down on paper, shaping them into a story, and finally seeing our work published was magical. It wasn't easy, but it was incredibly rewarding.

That's when it hit me—there were so many people out there

with stories to tell, businesses to promote, and messages to share, but they didn't know where to start. I had been in their shoes before, uncertain of how to take that first step. That's when I decided to start offering book coaching to help others do what my husband and I had just done. And so, Pro Publishing House was born.

It wasn't just about writing a book—it was about crafting a legacy, a tool to amplify their voices, and a product that could turn their expertise into a bestseller. My experience in network marketing had taught me so much about the power of personal branding, storytelling, and building an authentic connection with people. I wanted to share that knowledge with others. I wanted to empower entrepreneurs, especially female entrepreneurs, to tell their stories in the most impactful way possible and to create something that could change their lives.

But I didn't stop there. My entrepreneurial spirit didn't just want to help people write books; it wanted to create a bigger impact. So, I also took the leap and created my own product brand, and—get this—my products ended up being sold in none other than London's Selfridges! It was an exciting moment, one of those "pinch me" times that reminded me that anything was possible if you had the right mindset and kept pushing forward.

Fast forward to today, and Pro Publishing House has become a place where aspiring authors come to turn their dreams into reality. I've had the privilege of working with hundreds of incredible women who have gone on to become best-selling authors in their own right. Whether they're using their books to elevate their business, share their expertise, or inspire others, the process has been one of immense growth and transformation for them—and for me.

I've always believed that women, especially entrepreneurs, have an incredible power within them to make an impact. But many of us just need the right support to unlock that potential. That's what I do every day. I work with passionate, driven women who want to share their message with the world. I help them navigate the ups and downs of writing, publishing, and marketing their books. And along the way, I get to witness their growth, their success, and their confidence soar.

Pro Publishing House isn't just about publishing books; it's about empowering people to become thought leaders, to position themselves as experts in their fields, and to step into the spotlight with their stories. It's about taking those years of wisdom, knowledge, and experiences and transforming them into something tangible that can change lives.

And the best part? I get to do it with joy, excitement, and a sense of fun. Business doesn't have to be all serious and stuffy. It can be fun, engaging, and full of creativity. And that's the energy I bring to everything I do—whether it's coaching a client on her book, brainstorming ideas for a new project, or celebrating someone's first best-seller.

Today, I help people create best-selling books that not only make a mark in the publishing world but also in the lives of readers. I've found my purpose in this space, and every day, I feel privileged to continue this journey, helping others achieve what I've done and more.

So, if you're thinking about writing your own book, or if you're an entrepreneur who's ready to take the leap and create something powerful, remember this: the journey may be full of challenges, but it's also full of rewards. And along the way, you'll discover a new version of yourself—one who's confident, empowered, and ready to share your story with the world. That's exactly what I'm here to help you do.

After all, we're not just creating books—we're creating legacies. And that, my friend, is the kind of fun that lasts a lifetime.

Top 10 Tips for Entrepreneurs Wanting to Write a Book and Become a Best-Selling Author

1. **Find Your Unique Angle** Your book needs to stand out in a crowded market. Identify your unique perspective or expertise that will offer value to your readers. Think about what makes your story, knowledge, or approach different from what's already out there. This will help you create a book that resonates with your target audience.

2. **Start with Your Why** Before you even put pen to paper, get clear on your why. Why do you want to write this book? How does it tie into your business and brand? Understanding the deeper motivation behind your book will help guide your writing process and ensure your message aligns with your business goals.

3. **Plan Your Book Like a Business** Treat your book like a business project. Create a roadmap: Set deadlines, establish milestones, and treat writing like

a priority rather than a side project. This will help you stay disciplined and on track as you progress toward completing your book.

4. **Write for Your Audience, Not Yourself** It's tempting to focus on what you want to say, but your book should be written with the reader in mind. Ask yourself, "What problem does my reader have, and how can my book provide the solution?" Always focus on providing value and solving a real-world issue that resonates with your target audience.

5. **Break It Down into Small Tasks** Writing a book can feel overwhelming, but it doesn't have to be. Break the process into manageable chunks. Start with an outline, then tackle each chapter or section one at a time. Small steps lead to big results, and consistency is key.

6. **Leverage Your Existing Network** As an entrepreneur, you likely already have a strong network of followers, clients, and customers. Use them! Share your book progress on social media, engage with your audience, and ask for feedback during the writing process. Not only will this keep you motivated, but it can help you build buzz and anticipation around your book before it's even finished.

7. **Create a Professional Publishing Plan** Whether you decide to self-publish or go the traditional route, it's crucial to understand the process of publishing. Plan ahead for editing, cover design, formatting, and distribution. You don't need to do everything

yourself, but assembling the right team of professionals can make your book shine.

8. **Develop a Strong Marketing Strategy** A great book is only effective if people know about it. Start thinking about your marketing plan before you publish. Create a website or landing page for your book, build an email list, and engage on social media. Consider creating a launch plan that includes pre-orders, giveaways, and promotions to generate buzz and drive sales.

9. **Get Reviews and Endorsements Early** Reviews are vital for a book's success. As you near completion, seek out early readers who can provide feedback and write reviews for your book. Positive endorsements from influencers or well-known figures in your industry can give your book a boost, especially when you're aiming for best-seller status.

10. **Believe in Your Book's Potential** Confidence is critical. Even when you hit roadblocks or feel unsure about your writing, believe in the value your book brings. You're not just writing for the sake of it—you're creating something that can change lives, elevate your brand, and position you as a thought leader. Keep pushing forward, and don't doubt your ability to make it a best-seller.

By following these tips, you'll not only write a book but also set yourself up for success as a best-selling author. Remember, writing a book is a journey that requires consistency, patience, and a clear vision. When you take the time to plan and execute, the rewards—both personally and professionally—will be worth every effort. Let your book be a reflection of your expertise, and a powerful tool to grow your business.

The Best-Selling Author Academy and Empowering Others to Build Their Own Publishing Companies

When I started Pro Publishing House, it was all about helping people write and publish books. But as time went on, I realised something: the world of publishing was changing. The traditional publishing routes weren't the only path anymore, and aspiring authors wanted more control over their work. I began to see an even bigger opportunity—not just to help people become authors but to empower them to build their own publishing empires.

And that's how the Best-Selling Author Academy was born.

I had always known that my strength wasn't just in writing or coaching—it was in seeing potential and helping others realise that they, too, could achieve greatness. The Academy became an extension of this vision. It wasn't just a place for people to learn how to write books; it was a space where entrepreneurs could take charge of their own publishing journey and create their own brands.

I'd seen it all too often—people with incredible stories to tell, yet unsure of how to get started, how to position themselves as experts, or how to take control of their own publishing destiny. The Academy is my response to that need. It's a platform for authors to learn not just how to write a book but how to build a business around it, how to market it effectively, and how to scale their expertise into something that stands the test of time.

Through the Academy, I teach women—especially women entrepreneurs—how to leverage their books as the powerful marketing tool they are. Writing a book can be the cornerstone of a thriving business, whether you're using it to attract clients, build authority, or inspire others. But what people often overlook is the publishing part. It's not just about writing the book, it's about how you present it to the world. And that's where I come in.

I've seen firsthand how a well-positioned, strategically marketed book can change everything for an entrepreneur. A book can help you become the go-to expert in your field, build your personal brand, and create new opportunities that you never even dreamed of. Whether it's being invited to speak at events, landing partnerships, or increasing your revenue, a book is often the key that opens those doors.

That's where the Academy takes things a step further. I don't just help people become best-selling authors—I teach them how to build a sustainable business around their book. From understanding your target audience to creating a brand that speaks to them, from mastering book marketing to learning how to turn your book into a product that sells, the Academy is a step-by-step guide for anyone looking to turn their book into a profitable venture.

But it's not just about the individual authors. I also teach people how to start their own publishing companies. I know it might sound ambitious, but trust me—when you have the right tools, knowledge, and mindset, anything is possible. Over the years, I've worked with women who've gone on to launch their own publishing companies. And seeing them take that leap has been one of the most fulfilling aspects of my work.

It's not just about putting words on paper—it's about creating a system. A system where you can publish books for others, build a catalogue of works, and establish a reputable brand in the publishing world. There's something incredibly empowering about knowing that you're not just helping yourself, but you're helping other authors get their voices heard, too.

Through the Academy, I break down the steps to launching a successful publishing company. It starts with understanding the industry, learning about the various aspects of publishing (from editing and design to distribution and marketing), and developing a clear vision for your business. I've been able to guide women through this process, showing them how they can take the knowledge they've gained and turn it into a thriving publishing house of their own. The ability to help others realise their dream of becoming a published author is incredibly fulfilling, and being part of that journey is something I hold close to my heart.

The beauty of the Academy is that it's not just about me teaching—it's about creating a community. The women who join the Best-Selling Author Academy are more than just students—they're part of a network of like-minded individuals, all working toward the same goal. Whether it's through mastermind groups, coaching calls, or collaborative projects, the Academy is a space where authors help authors, and where publishing businesses help each other grow.

There's power in unity. There's power in creating something with a group of people who share your vision. And that's exactly what the Academy provides: a platform where you can learn, grow, and connect with others who understand your dreams and challenges. I've seen women who started out unsure of themselves and their writing abilities blossom into confident, best-selling authors, building not just books but businesses that last.

Looking back on my own journey—from network marketing to book coaching, from publishing my first book to launching the Best-Selling Author Academy—there's one thing that stands out: the power of stories. We all have them, and they all deserve to be shared. But the impact of those stories doesn't stop with the book itself—it extends far beyond that. It's about creating something bigger than yourself, building a platform for others, and making a difference in the world.

Whether you're an aspiring author, an entrepreneur looking to leverage your book for business growth, or someone dreaming of creating your own publishing company, the possibilities are endless. And with the right tools, knowledge, and guidance, you too can become a best-selling author and a successful publisher.

At the end of the day, it's not just about the book—it's about the legacy you leave behind. And in my world, there's nothing more exciting than helping others create a legacy that'll last for generations to come.

This is just the beginning. Whether you're writing your first book or launching your own publishing house, I'm here to help you turn your dreams into reality. Let's make it happen—together.

Connect with me:

Facebook: www.facebook.com/traceymunro12/

Instagram: www.instagram.com/traceymunro/

Website: www.propublishinghouse.com

**"WHISPERS OF DOUBT ARE LOUD ONLY
TO THOSE WHO CHOOSE TO LISTEN."**

Tracey Munro

GRIT AND GRACE

CHARITIES OUR AUTHORS SUPPORT

Women's Aid is the national charity working to end domestic abuse against women and children. As a federation we provide life-saving services across England while building a future where domestic abuse is not tolerated. **www.womensaid.org.uk**

Purchase any of the following books below to fund epilepsy information packs for schools.

www.amazon.co.uk/Jos-Hidden-Secret-Emma-Louise-James/dp/191528810X

www.amazon.co.uk/Jos-Hidden-Secrets-Emma-Louise-James-ebook/dp/B0D362M8RV

Widnes Gymnastics Academy (WGA) At WGA, talent, hard work, and resilience matter more than background or circumstances. It's a place where young gymnasts are given the opportunity to compete at the highest level, including the World Gymnastics Championships in Las Vegas, proving that anyone can achieve when given the chance. As a registered charity, WGA relies on funding to keep these dreams alive. But talent alone isn't enough; without financial support, opportunities are lost. That's why I'm backing WGA. Because grit and grace don't just belong in gymnastics—they shape future champions in life. **Every donation** makes a difference. **www.widnesgymnasticsacademy.co.uk**

If you wish to donate to Mary's Place®

www.justgiving.com/crowdfunding/MarysPlace2024

GRIT AND GRACE

NOTES

NOTES

NOTES

NOTES

NOTES

NOTES

NOTES

GRIT AND GRACE

Printed in Great Britain
by Amazon

59334846R00119